P₁

Suicide Prevention /

"Trudy Carlson has done her ~~*home*~~ MW01077348
and suicide is long overdue in our culture. Only when we ... _
what Carlson understands will suicide be prevented." *Mary Kluesner,
Chairperson, SA\VE*

"Trudy Carlson shares a compelling family journey of struggle and love.
This book impacts us with the seriousness of childhood depression and
the tragedy of suicide. "*Marilyn Koenig, Friends For Survival*

"My brother was thirteen when he died. There were so many parallels
with Dennis' life, I felt that I was reading about him. I look forward to
any other books you will publish. You do wonderful work!" *Tracy
Pierson, woman who lost her brother to suicide*

"An honest document which brings childhood depression and suicide out
of the closet." *Carole Katz, Regional Coordinator - Compassionate
Friends and author of Laurie, Laurie, Hallelujah!*

Health Care Professionals
"A beautiful example of parent insight, dedication, and understanding.
My hearty endorsement and gratitude for this book." *Jerome Kwako
M.D., Pediatrician; Director, ADHD Clinic, Miller Dwan Hospital*

"I have read your books with interest and compassion. I want to
compliment you for fine efforts to spare others from what you and your
husband have been through." *Dr. Mogens Schou, Riskov, Denmark,
pioneer in the use of lithium therapy for manic-depressive illness*

Teachers
"Finally, someone who understands. This is not only Ben's story; this is
also Ben's mother's story. All of the fears and anxieties a parent feels
are addressed in this book -- before, during and after diagnosis and
suicide." *Vicki M. Bresson, SA\VE Board Member, Former Teacher.*

"An open-hearted, detailed account of one mother's struggle with the
death of her son. I was struck by the enormous effort it takes to care for
someone with an illness such as Ben's." *Robin Blatnik, M.A.E.S.,
English and Composition Instructor*

II

Ben's Story:

The Symptoms of Depression, ADHD, And Anxiety That Caused His Suicide

By Trudy Carlson

FIRST EDITION

Benline Press, Duluth Minnesota

Publisher's Note

The information in this book regarding illness is intended to raise the awareness of the symptoms of depression, attention deficit hyperactive disorder, and anxiety disorder in young people, as well as the potentially effective treatments for these conditions. It is not a substitute for the advice and directions of your personal physician. It is not meant to encourage anyone to take any medications or make changes in the way current medications are taken without first consulting your doctor.

Copyright 1998 by Trudy Carlson M.S.

ISBN 096424436-5 Library of Congress No. 96-083889

Benline Press, 118 N. 60th Avenue East
Duluth, Minnesota 55804

Publisher's Cataloging in Publication Data
Carlson, Trudy M
Ben's Story: The Symptoms of Depression, ADHD, and
Anxiety That Caused His Suicide
Includes bibliographical references and Index
1. Children -- Suicidal behavior
2. Child psychology
3. Depression in children
4. Attention-deficit-disordered children
5. Manic-depressive illness in children
96-083889
09642443-6-5

TABLE OF CONTENTS

VI

Appendix 1

I Screening instrument for Fourth - Sixth grade

II Recommended curriculum for 7th - 12th Grade

A. For Parents, Teachers, and Health Professionals

B. Especially for Health Professionals

Appendix 2

ACKNOWLEDGMENT

No book is the product of just one person. My heartfelt gratitude goes to everyone who contributed to it. I want to thank those individuals who read this work in manuscript form at various stages. They include: Roseann Biever, Caroline Carlson, Lu Harter, Char Gallian, Margaret Kinetz, Monica Natzel, Carol Nord, Rod Nord, Jo Stewart, Nancy Scheftner, Dr. Elisabeth Kubler-Ross, Dr. Barry Garfinkel, Dr. Kenneth Irons, Dr. Jerome Kwako, Carol Michaelson, Eileen Gannon and Dr. Carrie Borchardt.

I would like to make special mention of Kristen Oberg, Patt Jackson and Robin Blatnik, the editors of the book, whose skill and encouragement helped to make it what it is. Their sustained commitment to this project is the kind of help writers dream of receiving, but never expect to get.

I wish to express appreciation to all the works that are quoted in this book. The list of these are contained in the bibliography.

There can be no full accounting of the debt I owe to the scores of people who contributed to this project by giving me advice and/or technical assistance. They include: Dr. Aaron Beck, Dr. Kenneth Broman, Joseph Gallian, Sheldon T. Aubut, Melanie Horn, Mary Kluesner, Marilyn Koenig, Tracy Pierson, Vicki Blesson. Special thanks to my brothers and sisters who helped in a number of ways.

The cover is designed by David Garon, and the painting on the cover is by Garry Carlson

Preface

On May 31, 1989 Benjamin Drew Carlson, aged fourteen, killed himself. In 1995 The Suicide of My Son: A Story of Childhood Depression was published. The book is both the story of Ben's life and the story behind the story. Part I shows how his depression, ADHD, and anxiety disorder manifest at various stages of his life, from infancy to adolescents. Part II gives the scientific information on the symptoms, treatment of depression and anxiety, and fact about suicide in the young.

Response to this book has been favorable. When this book has been displays at conferences for parents, teachers, counselors and therapists, a frequent comment is that people like to have books that are light weight, easy to pick up, carry in a purse or brief case. Consequently, while continuing to publish the original volume, the decision was made to also present it as two separate, smaller books. Part I is now published as Ben's Story: The Symptoms of Depression, ADHD and Anxiety that Caused His Suicide. Part II is now published as Depression in the Young: What We Can do to Help Them.

Introduction

When young people kill themselves the question always arises: Why did they do it? What happened in their short time on earth to lead them to take such a step? Before my own son's death, I was naive about such matters. I thought it must be the parents' fault. The parents must have failed their child in some awful way. They had not provided the young person with a solid basis on which to build his or her life. They missed some essential element to give the children what they needed.

After my son Ben's death in 1989, my husband and I began attending a suicide grief support group. There I met many dedicated, loving parents. I can honestly say many of them fit the description of model parents. They provided the kind of home any child would want.

One mother shared this comment made to her at her son's funeral. A friend said, "Your son's death frightens all of us. You and your husband are such good parents. If something like this could happen to your family, then none of us are safe." Is this true? Do all parents have to worry about their own sons or daughters committing suicide?

After my son's death I did a lot of reading about suicide. I wanted to know what is behind the suicide in young people. I wanted to discover the profile of the type of youngster who takes his own life. I learned that, for the most part, some type of illness, often a depressive condition, usually is involved in the suicide. Most frequently, the depressed young person who dies has at least one other additional problem. It could be depression plus an anxiety disorder, or depression plus chemical dependency, or depression plus an attention deficit hyperactive disorder. It can be depression alone, but two or more conditions increase the risk.

In my son's case it was bipolar illness (manic-depression). This condition caused his moods to swing from manic highs to depressive lows. Ben also had an attention deficit hyperactive disorder (ADHD) which prevented him from being able to pay attention to his teachers and from completing regular classroom routines. Ben also had seasonal affective disorder -- low mood, low energy during the cold months of the year when there is less sunshine. There is reason to believe he had dysthymia -- chronic low mood. Ben also had an anxiety disorder that caused him to have panic attacks. All of these conditions will be explained more fully and exemplified by his life story.

Ben's various medical conditions may lead you to think that it should have been obvious that something was wrong, but it was not obvious to anyone. He was a boy with a ready smile who liked adults and was liked in return. His problems with school work were regarded as a lack of motivation and poor study habits by his teachers.

I asked these questions: How do the symptoms of a depressive illness manifest at various stages in a child's life? Which of Ben's symptoms were caused by the depression, which by anxiety, which by the attention deficit hyperactive disorder, and what was the overlap? Psychologist and author, Rollo May, has written that one does not write because one knows the truth, one writes to discover the truth. I wrote to discover the answers to my questions; I wrote not only to resolve them in my own mind, but give some insight to the teachers, parents, health professionals, and suicide survivors who will read these pages.

The reader will see how, in infancy, Ben's life shows two of the hallmarks of depression -- problems with sleeping and eating. His preschool years demonstrate high-risk/accident prone behavior, the start of bedwetting (a common problem for depressed and anxious youngsters), and a feeling of discomfort when playing with others. Starting with elementary school, the attention deficit hyperactive disorder becomes a major issue. Here, Ben's inability to pay attention, his impulsivity, and his poor organizational skills are apparent.

Problems with thinking characterize both ADHD and depression. The child with ADHD has deficient thinking, while the depressed child has distorted thinking. Separating examples of deficient thinking (not planning ahead or seeing the consequences of their actions) from distorted thinking (nobody likes me, I never do anything right, I never have any fun) are not easy when the child has both conditions.

Ben's elementary years demonstrate his inability to function in the distraction-rich environment of a typical classroom. They illustrate his frustration (and my own) with a condition not understood by school personnel. I am sure many other parents have similar frustrations. Likewise, many teachers would appreciate knowing what is wrong with the child in their classroom who has difficulty getting his or her work done.

In Ben's final years, coping with the transition to adolescence (a task all youngsters find challenging) was especially difficult. The social immaturity and the impulsivity associated with both bipolar illness (manic-depression) and attention deficit disorder made life painful as well as potentially dangerous. Ben's anxiety disorder added to his sense of "dis-ease." Experimenting with alcohol and drugs is almost a natural consequence of these conditions for the adolescent. Although there was no evidence of drug use by my son, I am not sure that the foundations were not there. Many parents whose child begins self-medicating may receive some insight into a possible cause for alcohol and drug use.

There has been a 300% rise in suicide among the young in the past few decades. Some current programs of prevention focus on the triggers for the act rather than the illness that underlies the death. This book is my attempt to raise the awareness of low cost methods that could treat the illnesses most often associated with suicide. I have a dream that one day young people in middle schools, high schools, colleges and technical schools will be offered elective classes that teach personal logic (thinking skills) and interpersonal social skills. Young people must possess proficiency in these areas if they are to be productive adults. Cognitive and social support training could effectively treat the symptoms of mild and moderate depression. This class should also include a component that teaches young people how to cope with anxiety, the other common and serious risk factor for suicide.

When simple and generally applicable programs such as these are used, the cost of highly sophisticated, expensive testing procedures may not be required. Youngsters get help and support rather than a diagnosis. Most knowledgeable and dedicated child and adolescent psychiatrists readily admit that the financial cost of diagnosis is high. Few parents can afford it, and it does not necessarily result in getting any helpful treatment for the child. What everyone wants is for young people to get the training and support they need.

We have witnessed great advances in medical care over the past years. Doctors are now able to save many infants who otherwise would have died. Older Americans are living active, healthy lives well into their seventies and eighties. The adolescent population, on the other hand, is the only segment of our society who has not had an improvement in health during the last 30 years. It has been said that child and adolescent psychiatry is fifteen years behind adult psychiatry.

Depression has been called the number one health care problem in the world. If we are finally going to do something about helping this under-served population, the students in all schools throughout our country, perhaps our first step is to recognize the signs of depression in the young. As one of the most common of all health problems, depression touches the lives of all of us. If this medical condition is seen objectively and not as a reason for guilt for either the student or the parents, it may be treated with little need for defensiveness.

I hope these pages will provide teachers with some insight into children who have problems learning and give parents understanding of the symptoms of depression so that they might recognize them in their own children. It may help health professionals gain public support for the important work that needs to be done. Other survivors of suicide may get insights into their own child's situation.

The death of a child is painful no matter what the cause. Had I been a mother in the early 1940's who lost a child to infection, the advent of penicillin would seem like a miracle that came too late. The implementations of some inexpensive programs that work with the cognitive and social skills problems associated with depression and teach the techniques helpful to cope with anxiety <u>is</u> a miracle too late to help my child. It might not be too late for yours.

May 31, 1989

O n May 31, 1989, my son killed himself. Our much loved, very loving, difficult boy was gone. As I stood there looking down at Ben's body, my own body became infused with a message that said, "This was supposed to happen this day." I struggled to put into my head the knowledge I felt in my body; I desperately tried to make some sense out of it. Why was this supposed to happen? Why was it supposed to happen this particular day?

I had been all too painfully aware of Ben's depression, but I never thought he would take his own life. Nor did I see any reason for him to do such a thing on that particular day. It seemed in most respects to be a day like any other day. He had gone to school as usual. We had gone to work as usual. Nothing was out of the ordinary.

When I was a child my parents taught me that the day you are to die is established for you from the time of your birth. They said nothing in the world can be done to alter the appointed hour. They used to say, "When your time is up, your time is up." So when the powerful message came to me, filling me from head to toe stating, "This was supposed to happen this day," it was a type of validation of their teaching.

In the weeks and months that followed I often wondered what the purpose was of his dying on that particular day. Although I have thought about it much and have come up with several possibilities, as of this writing I do not have a clear answer to this question. I do, however, sense that something deep within myself and my husband was helping to prepare us for Ben's death. This preparation came to us in three separate forms: dreams, intuition, and anxiety.

Three or four days before my son died, I had a powerful dream that made a strong impression on me. It was very simple: I had breast cancer and was going to die. When I awoke I knew this was important and I gave it careful consideration. I wondered if it was a statement about my health or if it was symbolic of something else. I thought about the feeling of the dream; the impression it produced was fear. I awoke feeling terribly frightened about an upcoming death. I remembered thinking: this dream does not make any sense to me. I am feeling frightened by death, but I am not afraid to die. I did not know the full meaning of the dream, but my initial interpretation was of a fear of death.

Looking back at it now, I can guess at the symbolism. One of the associations I make to the symbol of breasts is "mothering and nurturing." I believe the dream helped prepare me for my son's death. Why does our unconscious find it necessary to prepare us for tragedies? I do not know, but it must serve a useful purpose. When Ben's death came I was understandably devastated by his suicide and surprised by it, but on another level I was prepared.

In the months since his death I have learned that when someone dies by suicide, the survivors are often filled with "If only..." regrets. I have read many stories written by the parents of children and young adults who took their own lives. In describing the last days of their child's life, these parents often say "If only I had taken him (or her) to a therapist when I saw this behavior, I might have saved him (or her)." Although being in therapy does significantly reduce the risk of suicide, many depressed people commit suicide while under treatment for their condition. It is not clear to me that anything in the world can circumvent the appointed hour of one's death.

The day of Ben's death began like any other. It had been a happy time for me because I had taken some vacation time to work on a writing project. This day, however, I found myself working frantically and feeling anxious. I told my husband, Garry, of my high anxiety level when I saw him at lunch. I remember feeling like I was jumping right out of my skin, and I could not figure out why. The project seemed to be working out well and I was pleased with the results. I could not figure out where this anxiety was coming from and why there was so much of it. Garry suggested I stop working for a while, but I did not see how this would reduce my anxiety, so I continued working.

Garry also had a disturbing dream that day. In his dream he saw an image of guns pointed at someone's head. It was either his own head or Ben's; the dream was not clear. When Garry awoke, he temporarily forgot the dream and only later in the day was he able to recall it. Garry remembers feeling tired and out of sorts that morning but he could not understand why.

At 3:10 Ben came home from school as usual. I was concerned about his eating habits. Ben's after school snacks were consisting of high sugar foods. We tried hard to steer him away from this eating pattern, but he always returned to it. Ben was gaining weight from eating too much junk food. I had ignored the situation for some time but decided I should not let him continue the behavior. I went to have a talk with him.

He was in one of the back garages and I said, "Ben, you have got to stop doing what you are doing. You have got to stop eating junk and start eating nutritious food." He responded angrily saying, "Stop treating this as if it were a crime."

A few minutes later we were both in the house and this time I was angry. I said "Ben, you have to start taking care of your health." We had a short conversation. I expressed my concern that he devise some sort of plan for taking better care of himself. Ben became upset and weepy. His response to me was, "A lot you would care if something happened to me." His reaction, although understandable, made me even angrier. After all, if I did not care about him, what was I doing trying to help him? What had I been doing all these years but trying to help him? I said, "That's not true." My fears for his health turned to anger at times when he did not seem to be taking care of himself. This was one of those days when I was especially worried and when his anger triggered my own.

I had made previous arrangements to go to dinner with some friends, so I left shortly after our conversation. My husband stayed to talk with Ben who was angry with me and critical of himself. He made deprecating comments that began with "Just look at me."

I think Ben was beginning to despair about his weight. Every time his weight would stabilize or decrease he would feel hopeful, but each time it took a leap forward he became discouraged. I had tried to encourage him by telling him about research on habit control which suggests that people who persist in trying different approaches ultimately become successful. I told him he should not become discouraged just because he had not yet found a system which worked for him. But perhaps Ben was beginning to wonder if things were ever going to work out for him.

As Garry and Ben talked, the conversation turned to the subject of his homework. My husband asked Ben what he had to do. Ben said he had a lot of catching up to do and he could not do it. Garry encouraged him to give it a try. Soon after their talk, Garry had to leave the house to attend an evening meeting for work. He promised to check in on Ben later to see how he was coming along with his school work. Garry left the room to get Ben a can of pop, and when he returned, Ben was fairly calm. He asked what time Garry would be returning, and Garry told him it would probably be sometime around 7:15.

My friends decided to come back to my house to play a few hands of cards. We arrived home about the same time Garry was returning from his meeting. Garry informed me that Ben was missing. This had never happened before. We usually knew where Ben was. Because of his depression and anxiety, the only places he felt comfortable were at home, at the homes of a few close friends, at the horse stable where he volunteered, and at our family business -- a group home for handicapped adults. Since he was not at any of those places and he had never been missing before, we did not have the slightest idea of where to start looking for him.

When I asked if Ben's bike was missing, Garry went to our garage and found it indeed was gone. Ben never went off on his bike as many kids do; he felt uncomfortable out on his own. To take his bike and go to a friend's house would have been unusual behavior for him. Both my husband and I were feeling frightened, but we hoped Ben's absence only meant he had been defiant and had gone out rather than doing his school work. We had taught both of our children to leave a note on the kitchen table if they had gone someplace unexpectedly, but there was no reassuring note on the table. Garry and I decided to take a "wait and see" attitude towards Ben's disappearance. I started to play cards with my friends, and Garry went to mow the lawn. I was worried about Ben, but I tried to concentrate on the game. I told myself, "Well you had better start getting used to this. Lots of parents of teenagers do not know where their kids are every minute, and they do not know everything they do."

The topic of conversation at the card table turned to kids. One of my friends took out a newspaper article she was carrying with her. (Later she told me she did not know why she felt compelled to have me read this article; she just knew she should share it with me.) The article was addressed to parents who feel guilty about how their children behave and try to figure out what they did wrong. The author described how, paradoxically, some children with neglectful or abusive parents manage to overcome many disadvantages and became productive citizens, while other children with parents who did everything in their power to help them have difficulty managing their lives. The article emphasized the importance of genetics in explaining behavior. Persons with a fortunate genetic endowment can make use of the opportunities they are presented with, while those with unfortunate genetic make-up have difficulties no matter how supportive and helpful the families are.

As I read it I could barely keep back the tears. Sometime during those last few minutes I began to have a strong fear something terrible had happened. My guess was we would find our son in one of the back garages. He had been going out there often during the last weeks, and I feared we would find him in our old Volkswagen with his wrists cut.

While I played cards, my husband was cutting the lawn. At exactly the same time that I suspected Ben had hurt himself, Garry also had the premonition Ben might be dead. While mowing the grass he suddenly recalled the dream he had had earlier in the day in which there were guns pointed at someone's head. Garry stopped the lawn mower. His intuition also told him he would find Ben in the back garage. He thought Ben would be there hanging. Garry went to the back garage, but Ben was not there.

Garry then went down to check his studio in the basement of our group home next door. He saw the locked door had been kicked in, and Ben was lying on the floor. In the confused emotions of the moment, Garry thought if he hugged Ben and kissed him, somehow he could bring him back to life. If he could show Ben how much he loved him, Garry thought he could change things.

While playing cards with my friends, I heard someone staggering up the back steps. The sound was vaguely like the noise Ben made when he came bounding home. I hoped Garry had found Ben loafing and had sent him back to his room to do some schoolwork. As worried as I had been about Ben, I could not have cared less about his homework. I was so relieved he was coming back home that I literally jumped out of my chair, fully intending to embrace him and tell him how glad I was to see him. Instead, the sound was Garry stumbling in the back door, half fainting or in shock, stating "It's Ben!"

"Should I call 911?" I asked. He replied, "Yes." As I lifted the phone to call, Garry said he was going back to the studio. One of my friends volunteered to make the phone call so I could follow my husband. I told Garry I was coming, and he cried, "Don't come!" But I knew no one in the world could prevent me from seeing my son. Operating on instinct, I knew that if I did not see Ben as he was then, I might regret it for the rest of my life.

I followed Garry as he went back to his studio. Ben's body was lying on the floor. He had shot himself in the head. I felt very detached when I saw him. Feeling detached and numb is a fairly common reaction, I later learned. Perhaps it is the protection we need in an overwhelming situation like this.

For several reasons, I will always be grateful I saw Ben when I did. First of all, I received the very clear message "This was supposed to happen this day." I am not sure this would have come to me on such a deep and profound level except in the immediate presence of my son's body. Secondly, in my son's case, the damage done by the bullet was hidden from us when we looked at Ben lying on his stomach. If I had not seen him there myself I am afraid my imagination would have created a image far more horrifying than reality. Finally, with the two of us there with our son I turned to my husband and asked, "Do you blame me for this?" My husband answered "No," and said it in a way that made me know he meant it. Garry and I got it clear from the beginning that neither of us blamed the other.

I could have decided to blame myself for Ben's death. It was I who had spoken to him about his eating habits, producing his angry reaction and creating an argument between us. It was partly my attempt to discourage overeating which served as the trigger for his destructive behavior. Although my actions would not have triggered suicidal behavior in a child without a bipolar (manic-depressive) illness, it could in a youngster with that disease. Dr. Popper, a noted psychiatrist, described the anger and potentially destructive behaviors of bipolar kids in this way: Bipolar children may exhibit severe temper tantrums, approaching psychotic degrees of disorganization and releasing manic quantities of physical and emotional energy, sometimes with violence and property destruction. The major destructiveness of bipolar children...tends to occur in anger....The 'trigger' for temper tantrums for...bipolar children (is) limit-setting (e.g., a parental 'No').

There is an important distinction between triggering something and causing something. Ben's bipolar illness was the cause of his suicide. Twenty percent of people with this condition eventually kill themselves. As I mentioned in the introduction, Ben had several depressive conditions and a learning problem. The combination of these conditions put him at high risk for suicide. The trigger for his death probably was the pressures of unfinished school work and my conversation about his eating patterns. Neither my motherly concern for his physical health nor Garry's request that he try to do some of his homework are to blame for his death. They may have been a trigger, but not a cause. Garry's statement that he did not blame me for the suicide has helped tremendously to decrease any guilt I might have chosen to carry relating to my son's self-destructive behavior.

Garry and I were with Ben's body for only a minute or so when the police arrived. They allowed us to stay with the body for a time while they made some initial inquiries. After a while, they said it was time to leave the scene. We went to another part of the basement for more extensive questioning as to the details of the incident.

At one point I was called upstairs because my sister-in-law had come to the house to find out why the 911 squad was there. I informed her of the suicide, that I was basically O.K., but Garry might be going into shock. When I returned to the basement, the officer was also becoming concerned about Garry. The person who finds the body often has an additional burden to bear. Since it was evening, the police advised us to go to the hospital for some attention. He offered to drive us: I was grateful because I did not think it was safe for us to drive.

We were at the hospital for approximately an hour. Shortly after our arrival, one of Garry's best friends arrived to see if he could help. Our friend was willing to spend the night with us, at our home. As Garry's condition stabilized we left the hospital. When we arrived home, I knew I would not be able to sleep. I wanted to rest, but I knew Garry and I would feel alone in our bedroom. I put on a sweat shirt and sweat pants, brought pillows and quilts into the living room, and we spent the night there. In that big, open, living area of our home we rested and talked, but did not sleep.

I did not want to call my family in a neighboring state until the morning. By 6 a.m. I was still numb about what had happened, and I had not been able to cry. I very much wanted to call my mother and then each of my sisters and brothers to tell them the news; this ritual was very important to me.

After I completed the last call to my family, I called my friend who was with me the night before to let her know about Ben. Her intuition had already told her what had happened, and she said she would be over. She stayed with me most of the day. It was so good to be able to tell her everything that came into my mind. Having a friend who is supportive, honest, and nonjudgmental is a treasure. She let me bring up anything I wanted to say without minimizing its importance. Sometime in the afternoon I grew tired, so she left while Garry and I got a little sleep. After a brief nap we began to think of other people who should be notified, and we made more phone calls. Garry's family came over to help us get started with some of the many decisions we needed to make. Later, our minister came over to help us with some initial planning.

One of the most poignant things I recall during that first afternoon was the feeling that I desperately wanted the power to turn back the clock 24 hours and change what had happened. Although logically I knew it was impossible to do, on that day it seemed somehow it should be possible! It had only been one day. Surely there must be a way to make it Wednesday again at 3:00 rather than Thursday. If it were Wednesday again, and Ben had just come home from school, I could stop working and we could have a quiet talk. I could offer to make him a salad. Eating together, I wouldn't have gotten upset about the junk he was consuming. I could have stayed at home and had my friends over for cards rather than going out. Surely there must be some way to turn the clock back 24 hours. It could not be that hard to do! I was thinking emotionally rather than logically. Like Garry, I wanted magical power to bring my son back to life. Garry had thought he could do it by hugging Ben's lifeless body. I thought I could do it by turning back time. But neither of us possessed the magic to save our son.

We did not sleep the second night either. Garry and I spent the evening in the living room with our quilts. Somewhere in the middle of the night, it occurred to me I would never be happy again for the rest of my life. I would never again feel joy, for every potentially happy moment would be spoiled by the fact that Ben was dead. As quickly as this idea came to mind, a totally different perspective replaced it. I remembered my father, who had died eighteen years earlier. In many respects I felt closer to him now than I had when he was alive. I have chosen to have a relationship with him by appreciating all of his fine qualities, especially his wisdom. I feel I am able to sense this wisdom when I need it. I draw strength from his strength of character, his integrity. I began to realize that, after a time, this would also be possible with Ben. His bipolar illness was a great burden for him, causing an enormous amount of difficulty coping with life. But the other side of Ben was an extremely sensitive, wonderfully loving and unusually wise youngster. In my future relationship with my son, I would be able to receive the benefits of his sensitivity, as well as the love and wisdom he possessed. A question occurred to me: What more could any mother expect to receive from her son?

As daylight appeared, I remembered what the minister said about dealing with some of Ben's belongings. He told us how some people find it easier to pack up some things right away. Although I had not slept during the night, I had the energy to get up and start re-organizing Ben's room. I very much wanted it to look different. Part of the reason we were avoiding our own bedroom was because it was adjacent to Ben's room. If we were going to live in this house and sleep in our bed, we needed to change the way Ben's room looked. Garry and I dismantled Ben's makeshift desk, moved his bed to the other side of the room and put some of his things away. I wanted to take care of his room myself and then clean my own room. I felt a need to take some of the turmoil inside me and use it to put my house in order. I wanted to do many things myself, but when my niece came over to see how she could help, I was more than happy to give her the assignment of cleaning our daughter's room. Caroline, a college student, was in Germany at the time; we reached her by phone to give her the news of her brother's death.

I was not sure coming home for the funeral would be the right thing for her to do. When telling Caroline about Ben's death I made it clear she had the choice of either coming home or staying where she was. I did not want to protect her from the death or exclude her from the process, but I wanted to respect her right to deal with things in her own way and in her own time. I felt uneasy about her traveling home alone under these circumstances. I was relieved when she decided to stay where she was. It was an honest decision based on what was right for her. We decided we could have a small private ritual when she returned.

The employees of our group homes were concerned and wanted to be helpful. They concluded that the best service they could do for us was to make sure the business ran as efficiently as it could. I have always appreciated our loyal and trustworthy staff, but in times like this, I especially realized how blessed we are to have them.

Friday morning, Garry's sister and one of her friends went with us to the mortuary to make arrangements. It is amazing how many decisions one has to make at a time when they are hard to make! We first had to decide whether we wanted Ben to be buried or cremated. Whether or not we would ultimately choose to cremate Ben's body or not, I knew I wanted it embalmed. I feel strongly that it is helpful to spend a number of days with its presence in order to bring closure with the physical body and to give ourselves enough time to say good-bye. Because he was embalmed, we had some time before we would have to decide on the final disposition of his body. This was especially important to us because it gave us time to again contact our daughter in Germany to find out her wishes. Garry wants to be cremated when he dies, so we were leaning towards this for Ben as well. But we did not want to be rushed into this decision, for once made, it can not be undone.

Selecting a coffin was one of the hardest things we had to do. The funeral director knew this would be difficult for us, and tried to prepare us for it, but I do not know how anyone can be prepared for a huge room filled with coffins. Perhaps the coffins force you to realize in a deep level the reality of what has happened. It was an overwhelming experience, and I wanted to get out of there as quickly as possible.

From the funeral home we went to the church. The minister wanted to give us some time to talk about the suicide. I found this both painful and helpful. It gave us a chance to get used to talking while crying. In the months ahead, as we worked through our grief, it would be important to talk about what had happened and how we felt. We needed to learn to continue to talk while we cried. We needed to begin to feel unashamed of crying and hoped others would feel comfortable about it too. After discussing the death, the minister involved us in the planning of the funeral. I had strong opinions about the music. I wanted a lot of it: no solos, only full congregational singing. Although solos are beautiful, I did not want anyone to feel excluded at any time from participating in the process of our final farewell to Ben's spirit in song.

Everything takes longer to do than you think, and when we finally came back home my mom and one of my sisters had arrived from out of state. Some of our friends had arrived, too, and it was comforting to see them. The flood of food had also started. At the time I could not imagine ever wanting to eat again, but I also realized there would be need for all of this food as more family and friends arrived. Later that night, with Ben's room altered in appearance and my family staying with us, Garry and I finally returned to our bedroom and got at least a few hours of sleep.

We went to the mortuary on Saturday morning. We again contacted our daughter in Germany and with her help made the decision to have the body cremated and the ashes brought home in a crypt to be placed somewhere in our home. We brought some clothing for Ben, and gave them to the mortician. We made another trip to the funeral home in the afternoon to make the decision about whether to have an open or closed casket during the visitation. This was another time we did not want to be rushed and where the funeral director was very helpful. Earlier he had advised us to let them prepare the body as well as they could and then have us come in to view it before deciding on whether to have the casket open or closed. Since the last time we had seen Ben was shortly after his suicide, the mortician said it probably would be helpful to us in the weeks and months ahead to see him now in a more peaceful state. In his opinion, it would be healing for us, and I now agree with him completely.

There was some swelling of Ben's face, so he did look slightly different than he had when alive. As I looked down on his body this second time, I felt very little connection between it and my son's spirit. My sense was that this was the part Ben had discarded. I remember saying "That isn't my son. My son continues. That is only his shell." There is a lot of healing in knowing this.

Because of the slight swelling in his face, we felt everyone would feel more comfortable with a closed casket. With the coffin closed, I wanted a lot of pictures displayed along with some of the things which were important to Ben: the saddle we had bought for horseback riding, and the trombone he loved. I was glad we had two framed collections of family snapshots at our home. I had put this collection together the year before, as a Christmas present for myself and for Garry. It contained all of my favorite pictures of Ben at all stages of his life. We put these on pedestals on either side of the entrance to the casket area.

As friends gathered at our home that evening, I realize I needed to reach out to some of Ben's closest friends to see how they were reacting to his suicide. Whenever there is a sudden death, especially a suicide, there can be the feeling that maybe something could have been done to prevent it. We especially wanted to contact Ben's friends from the horse stable. We requested they come to our house because we wanted to reassure them that we cared about them, and they were not to feel responsible for Ben's death. Logically, of course, there would be no reason for them to feel responsible, but logic has little to do with this type of situation. In cases like this, most people end up feeling, "If only I would have called him that night and offered to do something with him he would not have been alone. If he wasn't alone, he probably wouldn't have killed himself." Everyone close to the deceased takes on unnecessary responsibility for the death.

The next day was Sunday. Around noontime the rest of my family arrived from out of state. Ben's depression had been unknown to them, so I explained a little about his illness. They had only known a boy who was outgoing with adults and who had a wonderful smile. Depressed young people often try to hide their pain and cope with life as best as they can. They try to overcome their illness and protect those around them from the burden of suffering. Ben's outward jovial appearance in social situations would not have led anyone to believe how terribly uncomfortable he often felt. It takes family and friends some time to accept the idea that here was a child who had a very powerful illness.

After explaining Ben's illness and our efforts to get appropriate medical attention, I found myself hungry for the first time in three days. After eating, it was time for the visitation. We had gathered still more pictures of Ben, which we put in individual plastic pages and took them to the mortuary. It felt good to see all of our friends and get all those hugs. I found the ritual associated with the funeral very helpful.

Monday was the funeral. You often read how family members experience some shame associated with a suicide death. I felt none the day of Ben's funeral. There almost seemed to be a military feel to the event, as if he were a fallen soldier. I think this came from knowing in my heart that Ben had tried his best to cope with his powerful illness, but it had overwhelmed him. It has been said that in a depressed state, the person will feel he or she is in a dark tunnel with no light on either end. I felt Ben had done the best he could for fourteen years. He had a genetically unlucky body, but within it lived a great spirit.

FOR BEN

Ben/
No answer.
Ben/
Where is that boy?

Ben has gone
a far journey.
A journey at once
familiar to all
and yet unfamiliar.

I believe this journey
ends in love.
As all things finally
end in love.
And that Ben now
knows what he could
only guess at.

Mark Arvilla
A Duluth Poet
Ben's friend

Infancy

After Ben's death, I found myself thinking back to the beginning of his life. It was enlightening to compare Ben's birth and infancy to that of our first child, Caroline. The birth of our daughter was a wonderful experience. I was thrilled about the pregnancy, and since she arrived the day before my own birthday, I felt she was the best present any woman could ever receive. I will never forget my reaction to her birth. My response to her was surprise: surprised that somehow this bulge in my body turned out to be a baby.

At the time, I was a twenty-seven year old instructor at the university teaching child development classes. I knew perfectly well this bulge was a baby, but there was nothing logical about my feelings of surprise. My reaction was an emotional one based on my being taken aback by the magic and wonder of life itself.

My second reaction came a day or two later, when Garry and I fell head-over-heels in love with this little creature.

We both commented how it felt as if we were fourteen years old again and had fallen in love for the first time. Her birth had the feeling of springtime, when the world is fresh and new. Our experience of loving this child was so special to us that we were convinced no other parents had ever loved a baby as much as we loved our beautiful daughter. This is total nonsense, but who ever said anyone in love is sensible?

The year was 1971 and doctors kept mothers in the hospital for five days. This delivery left me feeling physically exhausted. During the first four days of my hospital stay, I was glad to be taken care of and happy to have someone else tend my baby. By the fifth day, I was rested and ready to go home. When I took Caroline home she was on a regular four-hour schedule: she would sleep for three hours, and then there was the one hour in which to change her diaper, feed her four ounces of formula, burp her, and put her back to bed. She had this four hour cycle which included the infamous 2 a.m. feeding for about six weeks. After that she began sleeping through the night.

How different things were with the birth of Ben. I was just as happy about my second pregnancy as I had been about my first. I had wanted to become pregnant again when Caroline was eighteen months old, but because my husband was going through a career change and finances were a little uncertain, I had delayed getting pregnant for an additional year. Ben was very much the long-awaited, welcomed addition to our family. When I told Caroline that she was going to have a sister or a brother, I asked her what she would like to name the baby. She answered, "Betsy." We had many delightful talks about the new Betsy coming to live at our house.

I was due on Thursday, March 13. I felt that I had started labor on two separate occasions earlier that week, but it had stopped each time. On my due date I had an appointment with my doctor, and told him what had happened. I requested to be admitted to the hospital on the weekend so labor could be induced. He told me that he usually preferred to let nature take its course, but if I insisted, he would proceed with the induction. It seemed to me that the baby and I were ready, so I made admittance plans for Friday.

When I entered the hospital Friday evening, the atmosphere in the maternity ward was tense. It seemed every woman there was having some sort of complication. The first woman I saw was in labor prematurely. If it was determined that they could not stop the labor, chances were the baby would need to go to the infant intensive care unit. The next person I saw was a student in one of my classes. His wife was in labor with twins. The following day she had two daughters, one of whom had spina bifida. These newborns were taken very quickly from the delivery room to the intensive care unit.

My own process of being induced started all right, but was temporarily interrupted because several hospital personnel were needed to handle the care of the twins. The staff got back to me as soon as they could, and continued the medication that would induce labor. After a time, my doctor decided to break my water since that would assist the process. It was then he discovered Ben was coming shoulder first rather than head first. (Perhaps this was the reason the labor, which started twice earlier in that week, had stopped each time.) My physician told me he would have had to do something to assist the birth. The doctor repositioned Ben by pushing back on his shoulder, thus allowing him to came head first. The birth occurred very quickly after this.

When the doctor said "It's a boy!" I was surprised. After so many months of calling him Betsy, it took me a few minutes to get used to the idea. Also, since I spent the preceding three and a-half years with the identity of "a mother of a daughter," it was going to take me some time to get used to the change. I remember thinking, with amusement, "Not only is he a boy, but he is ugly." I do not know if it had anything to do with the days of waiting to be born or simply from the process of birth itself, but initially Ben did not look that great. Surprisingly, within five minutes, Ben's face sort of re-arranged itself and he turned into an exact replica of the baby I had had three and a half years earlier.

Later a nurse would take the receiving blanket off Ben's little body to show me he was perfect, with all ten fingers and all ten toes. A healthy beautiful boy: how lucky we were to have him! But my attention did not seem to be focused on my new son. I felt depressed and found myself crying in my room. Dr. Gold, an expert on mood disorders, tells us that "The vast majority of women (70 to 80 percent) endure `maternity blues.' Frequently, on the third day following delivery the new mother becomes tearful, sleepless, tense , and angry. Episodes come and go for twenty four hours to a week, then they lift" (Gold, p. 281). In my case, I was not unwilling to relate to my baby nor was I unhappy about his arrival. What I felt was overwhelming sadness about the fate of the babies born that day and sorrow for the mothers who bore them. I especially focused on the baby with spina bifida. I knew the parents, and because I had some experience with this condition, I was sorry for what they might go through in the future.

As I wept in my hospital bed, I cried for this new little baby girl with spina bifida, knowing it was possible this child would have the pain of growing up feeling different, sometimes excluded. Being different, even in cases where the differences do not seem great, can create a major gulf between a child and its peers. Sometimes the peer group may not even detect any difference, but if the child feels different, he will feel not quite at home in the world. In my hospital room I thought I was crying for this new little girl, for her pain, and the pain her parents would feel in the upcoming years as they saw her excluded from some of the simple joys of life.

How paradoxical life can be! Looking back on it now I see that although I was thinking about this little girl, what I really was seeing was a preview of my own son's life. It would be my son whose inability to concentrate would make it difficult to comprehend the strategies and rules of games like baseball and football. It would be my son who would feel "different". The "manic quantities of physical and emotional energy" associated with his bipolar (manic-depressive) illness would make it difficult for him to get along with or play easily with other children. His attention deficit hyperactive disorder (ADHD) and his anxiety disorder would also be a factor in these problems. His multiple problems would cause him to exclude himself or be excluded from many activities. It would be my heart that would break as I saw him being excluded. My efforts to find some way to help him fit into the mainstream would be frustrated.

The little girl born on that day died in a year. My son coped for as long as he could with a dysfunction created by a genetic condition. People with bipolar illness inherit a predisposition to the illness. Scientists are now trying to pinpoint the exact genetic marker for this disorder. Little by little, I would come to understand what it is to care for an infant with depressive illness.

On Ben's first full day home, I began to see that he did not have an easy schedule. He did not want to drink all of his formula, and he was not able to sleep for consistently long stretches of time. Eager to leave the hospital and get back home to my husband and daughter, I left the hospital sooner than I would have had to go. By the second day at home, I concluded I may have made a mistake rushing to get back. When I had stayed in the hospital five days with my daughter, I took home a baby who had an easy four-hour schedule. The nurses, I concluded, must know how to manage these newborns in a way that produced this pattern. Rushing Ben home early had not allowed the nurses time to produce the wonderful scheduling of three hours sleep and one hour feeding.

This would prove to be the first of many times I would conclude that Ben's difficult behavior was the result of something I had done, or failed to do. He was having problems eating and sleeping: two of the classical markers of depression. He showed these signs at four days old!

I hope I will not be misunderstood here. I am not saying that every baby who has trouble with eating and sleeping is going to grow up with bipolar illness. What I am saying is that my child had a genetic condition which affected him throughout his life, and it was marked enough for me to remember a warning sign which showed up at four days old. Also, the problems of people with bipolar illness are not a result of environment or rearing. Research indicates that children with bipolar illness generally have good mothering (Gold, 1987).

As the weeks went on, I tried to deal with Ben's eating and sleeping problems in a number of different ways. If I could get Ben to drink larger quantities of formula at a time, I thought he would sleep for longer periods. No matter what I did though, he would drink about two ounces of formula and fall asleep. I would jiggle the bottle back and forth to try to get him to suck, but it did not work. He would sleep for an hour or so and wake up hungry.

This frequent need to be fed occurred around the clock. Instead of a single 2 a.m. feeding, Ben required several nighttime feedings. Furthermore, this behavior did not stop after a month or two. As he got older he would drink more than just two ounces but continued to waken during the night throughout his babyhood. When he was six, seven, and eight months old I was still usually getting up once or twice during the night to give him a bottle.

Dr. Popper has observed that this is a common occurrence for infants with bipolar illness. In his article <u>Diagnosing Bipolar Vs ADHD</u>, (attention deficit, hyperactive disorder) he writes: "During infancy, certain bipolar children do not sleep through the night to establish an overnight sleep pattern until 8 - 12 months, or even until four years of age." I do not remember how old Ben was when he finally slept through the night. My guess is he was still waking once during the night past his first birthday. I would just hand him a bottle and stagger back to bed hoping to get more sleep. This continuous feeding had a negative effect on his new baby teeth, causing him dental problems later on.

I did all sorts of other things to help him sleep through the night. I tried a strategy that had worked when my daughter was an infant. When she was old enough to start eating cereal, I would give it to her late in the evening just before I wanted to go to bed myself. When I tried things like this with Ben, they did not work to help him sleep through the night. I even tried giving him a bath in the evening, knowing baths usually tire babies out, but nothing worked. The standard "just let him cry without feeding him" did not work, either. When I called my doctor in desperation for some help in getting this seven month old infant to sleep during the night, he suggested that I try putting a little decongestant into his bedtime bottle for a few evenings. He thought after a few nights a longer sleep pattern would develop. The decongestant did improve the condition, but no pattern developed. Without the decongestant, Ben did not sleep through the night.

By telling the story of Ben's life, I hope to illustrate that depression in children is the same as depression in adults, but the symptoms are slightly different. For example, depressed adults have sleep disturbances. Infants with depression may not sleep through the night. Depressed adults either do not eat enough or eat too much. Infants with depression are frequently underweight, or like Ben, have other eating problems. Depressed adults may have problems with constipation. Ben's difficulties with constipation began as an infant and continued throughout his childhood. Depressed adults can experience aches and pains in their bodies. As an infant, Ben usually cried each day for about an hour or so. Nothing I could do -- no amount of rocking him or walking with him -- succeeded in comforting him. I have often wondered about the source of his discomfort. I can not be sure it was caused by the depression, but it is certainly a possibility in view of the aches and pains he reported later in childhood. ADHD children also may show signs of agitation as babies, so not all of Ben's fussiness in infancy may have been caused exclusively by his bipolar illness, but the eating and sleeping problems probably were.

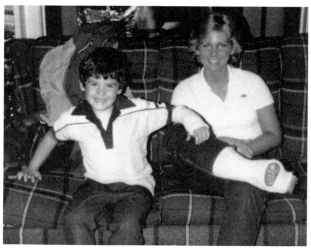

Preschool

Much of this chapter describes Ben's impulsive, dangerous behaviors. Children with attention deficit hyperactive disorder are predominately characterized by impulsivity which sometimes results in posing a danger to themselves. Describing what life was like for Ben in his preschool years helps to make the connection between these dangerous behaviors during those early years and his impulsive, self-destructive act of May 31, 1989.

Ben started to walk at twelve months and was a very active youngster from that point on. The terrible two's started for Ben at eighteen months, when he began climbing out of his crib. Ben was determined to get out of his crib and did not seem to care if he got hurt in the process. I decided it was better to lower the side of the crib and let him climb out safely rather than risk injury.

Our children were sharing a room in the two bedroom house we lived in at the time. Now that Ben was no longer confined to his crib, our five year old daughter, Caroline, was not able to play without Ben disrupting her activities. An inability to play quietly and cooperatively with others is typical of toddlers, but Ben was particularly difficult. To reduce friction between the children, we purchased bunk beds. Caroline could then play on the top bunk if she wished to get away from Ben's interference. We bought the beds, set them up and felt everyone had a way to relax.   My relaxing was to come to an end exactly one week later. I was resting on the bottom bunk and keeping Ben company while he played in the room. Caroline was on the top bunk. I had my eyes closed and was enjoying the relative peace and quiet when I heard Caroline say, "Good Ben, you climbed up here". My eyes shot open. My eighteen month old had climbed up the back of the bunk bed and was now on the top. I grabbed him and put him on the floor, but once again he climbed up the back of the bunk bed. That night my husband and I lifted the top bunk off and the children ended up with two single beds.

So, at eighteen months, Ben was in a regular bed and not confined in any way. This would not have been a problem if it were not for his tendency to engage in dangerous behaviors. For example, Ben often put things into electric outlets. We bought plastic plugs to put into the receptacles. Ben would just remove the plugs and proceed to put things into the outlets. He received shocks a number of times; I once saw sparks come out of a socket. Ben cried, obviously in pain, but he continued to poke his finger and other things into the light sockets. It was not as if we did not tell him "no" and move him away from the wall, but Ben was a very determined little boy.

Another of his favored play areas was the stove. From his age of one-and-a-half to three-and-a-half, I never used the oven because Ben wanted to open the door and crawl in. I needed to be sure the oven was not only off, but cool. Recently, my daughter told me a story about little Ben which dramatizes my need for caution regarding the oven.

One night when we were out, the baby-sitter became terrified because she could not find Ben. She and Caroline ran around the house looking for him. The sitter went down to the basement twice looking for Ben. The second time she came back up and walked through the kitchen she heard a knock coming from the oven. Looking through the glass on the door she saw

Ben's little face smiling at her. She screamed! Apparently Ben had discovered that after he climbed into the oven it was possible for him to hit the door with his hand in such a way that the door would close behind him. Can you imagine what would have happened if she have decided to heat the oven to make a pizza?

Ben also loved the burners on top of the stove. Twice he took pans of boiling water off the burner. We were always careful to put pans on the back burners with the handles pointed in, but Ben would then grab the side of the pan. The first time he did this he received a small burn on his arm. It formed a blister about the size of a quarter. The second time he did not get burned at all. The boiling water went all over the floor but it missed Ben completely. Once when he was small, I ran down to the basement to quickly put a load of clothes in the washer. I returned to find him sitting on a burner playing with the knobs. Luckily, again, he was not burned.

Finding ways to safely confine Ben for the times we could not watch him took much effort and time. We hit on the idea of cutting off the top part of his bedroom door, making it into a Dutch door. His room then would become something of a large play pen. At eighteen months, Ben could climb out of a regular sized play pen, but until he mastered the art of turning knobs, he would be safe playing in his room. He could look out over the top of the door and not feel shut in. We could check up on him and know that he was all right.

A year later we moved to a new three bedroom house. The property on which we built our house had a log cabin playhouse in the backyard. During the next year I furnished the playhouse with a 9 x 12 foot rug, a small bed, a combination oven and sink, and an old chair. I put an old shelving unit in one corner and added lots of discarded dishes. Some of them were little plastic plates and bowls, but I also had some glassware. I had thought of just throwing away those mismatched glasses, but standing with them in my arms poised over the garbage can, I thought about the playhouse and decided my daughter would enjoy playing with them. I had furnished the playhouse with my seven year old daughter and her girl friends in mind. I was not thinking about little boys.

One afternoon, when four year old Ben was playing a little too quietly with the three year old neighbor boy, I thought I should investigate. When I opened the door to the playhouse, Ben was standing with a croquet mallet poised high above his head, about to smash a glass. The rug was totally covered with broken glass. The neighbor boy was watching.

My thought was, "If either of those boys fell, they would be cut from head to toe!" I told them both to freeze. First I grabbed the neighbor boy and took him out of the playhouse. Then I grabbed Ben and took him out. I told the neighbor to go home and Ben to go to his room. I then cleaned up all the broken glass, removed the few remaining unbroken glasses, and put them all in the garbage. I knew I had to impress upon Ben the dangerous nature of what he had done. What was I to do to help him understand? I can not remember all that I did, but it included a long, serious talk.

Some parts of Ben's preschool years had not been that different from Caroline's. Both my children had been very active with a general lack of interest in quiet activities such as coloring or putting puzzles together, but there were definitely differences between them. Caroline tried to include Ben in her games and he tried to fit into them, but there were always problems. She had been in several family daycare settings as a young child where she played with a number of children. Caroline also played in her neighborhood "gang." She says Ben was the type of kid one could not play with. She described how Ben would get to a certain point where he would just lose control. He would become overly excited, or overly aggressive, or overly sensitive, or tearful. In one way or another, he would be disruptive of their play. After a time, Caroline and her friends concluded that it was just easier to exclude him, and they avoided playing with him.

A neighbor of ours has said nearly the same thing. Ben would often go to her house to play. Her children would play with him for a time, but the outcome of their games would always be the same: Ben would end up feeling hurt and would return home in tears. Ben had an overly-sensitive nature and an enlarged reaction to everything. He was an active child, but it was not wild hyperactivity in which the child is constantly in motion and disruptive. It was more like an intensive reaction to specific situations. When he was having a good time, he would become too exuberant and silly. When he was angry, he would get furious. Ben cried easily and often. Sometimes when his crying was especially long and hard, he would vomit.

During the period between age two-and-a-half and three-and-a-half, Ben did not seem to develop many new skills. I remember thinking "he was a year older and a year bigger, but developmentally he was about the same as he was a year earlier." Ben also had a peculiar speech habit: whenever he would say anything, he would mouth the last few words of the sentence silently a second time. (Other signs of speech/sentence structure peculiarities would show up later.) I now know that both slowness in processing information and speech can be a sign of depression.

As Ben got older and was involved in nursery school and kindergarten, he continued to display dangerous behaviors. He had three injuries during the 18 month period starting from February 1980 to August 1981, the periods from when he was not quite five years old until just past his sixth birthday.

At dinner one evening we were finishing our meal and discussing what was for dessert. Ben knew we had some ice cream in the freezer unit on the top portion of our refrigerator. Impatient for the rest of us to finish our meal before dessert was served, Ben climbed to the top of the counter to get a dish for the ice cream. Perched there, he was also in a position to open the freezer unit. Suddenly he lost his balance and tumbled to the floor. He was crying as I picked him up, and he said his head hurt. I comforted him as much as I could, but he was in a lot of pain.

The next morning his head was fine, but when I dressed him he winced as I put on his shirt. He pointed to a place on his shoulder that hurt. I sent him to the sitter as usual. At dinner he still reported pain in his shoulder. Later that night I was with some friends, and I told them what had happened. I made light of the situation, as the latest of many experiences with this boy who was continually getting into trouble. My friends were concerned about the pain in Ben's shoulder, and they suggested I take Ben to the doctor. The next day Ben cheerfully gave the doctor an account of his adventure climbing the counter to get himself some peppermint bon-bon ice cream. It was obvious to me how charmed both the doctor and his nurse were by this spunky little boy who enjoyed talking with adults.

An x-ray confirmed what my doctor suspected, a broken collar bone. My reaction was "Oh my God, he's had a broken bone for almost two whole days, and I have ignored it by not getting treatment for it." I felt terrible about this. My doctor immediately became surprisingly firm with me, telling me to stop all this guilt business. It was uncalled for and not appropriate in this case. He reassured me that a slight delay in getting treatment is no reason for feeling guilty, and would have no negative affects. I was taken aback by the strength of the statement in this generally mild-mannered, cheerful man. I was also deeply grateful to him. Ben wore the little shoulder brace for six weeks, and the shoulder healed just fine.

About six months later, Caroline got a new two wheel bike for her birthday. Ben wanted to try riding it and Caroline let him. I sat on the front steps outside my home watching all of this. I told Ben he was too young to ride the bike, but if he promised to stay on the large blacktop area in front of the garage or ride it on the lawn he could ride if for a short time with supervision.

It was such a pleasure to watch them. It did my heart good to see Caroline willing to share her new bike with her little brother, especially since Ben had difficulty playing with other children. Ben was thrilled, and I was thoroughly enjoying myself when the phone rang and I went inside the house to answer it. Caroline and her playmate also needed to go into the house at that time. Ben saw his chance to take the bike out onto the sidewalk. Our neighborhood is on a slight incline. If Ben rode down the sidewalk he would be able to go pretty fast. This would be a lot more exciting than just going around and around in circles on the blacktop as I had asked him to do. The fact that the blacktop or grass would make a softer landing than concrete for a child learning to ride a bike apparently was not an issue with Ben.

I was talking on the phone when I suddenly heard an ear piercing cry. It would be years before I would actually find out all the details of what happened, but Caroline tells me that the front wheel of the bike hit a lead pipe on the land between the sidewalk and the street. When Ben fell off the bike, his head hit the sidewalk. The girls heard Ben crying and ran out to see what had happened. They brought him into the house with a very sore head.

The next morning Ben was still reporting some pain, so I called the doctor. I told him that as Ben cried about the pain, he would become very upset and vomit. The doctor wanted to know if Ben often vomited when he cried hard. As I mentioned earlier, many typical day-to-day events would set Ben off emotionally into crying long and hard, which sometimes did cause him to vomit. The doctor felt Ben probably had a concussion from the fall, but there was not much we could do. Ben's head would hurt for a week or so, and we would see some vomiting during that time. Rest and time was the only treatment for the injury.

About a day later, the top and back of his head began to feel soft, and I panicked. What if Ben did not simply have a concussion? My fear was that he might have some other, more serious, injury. I did not know what was wrong, but I suspected the worst when I felt his soft head. I again called my doctor.

The softness was probably caused by blood collecting between the skull and the scalp. The doctor said Ben's body would naturally absorb it over time, and we would just need to wait for the process to occur on its own. In a kindly, nonjudgmental way, he indicated that since ice was not applied at the time the injury occurred, there really was not anything we could do now except wait for it to go away.

As the days went by, I kept feeling the back of Ben's head. It seemed to be getting softer. This was also Garry's impression. I was trying not to panic or be upset, but that is easier said than done. During the weekend I had lots of time to observe Ben's head and lots of time to worry. At the end of two days of non-stop fear, I took Ben to the emergency room to have them check it. Just going through the process of once again talking about the injury with medical personnel seemed to relieve the pressure of my concern. They reassured me that there was not anything abnormal about the swelling, and since it was not a new injury there was not anything they could really do to help me. Nor could they give me any answers to my concern that Ben's head seemed to have gotten a bit softer in the last couple of days. They were sympathetic and told me it would likely take a few more days before we would begin to see absorption of the blood. They were very polite, but a little confused as to why I was bringing an old injury to the emergency room. My answer to this was that there are probably few things that are quite as unnerving as to have the back of your child's head feel like a marshmallow. To our relief, a few days later the swelling did go away.

The following June, Ben had his third accident. He had just finished kindergarten and it was the first day of summer vacation. I was out of town at an all day meeting. I got home around 6 p.m., but there was no one around and this made me a little nervous. The doors were open, the windows were open, and there was no note on the kitchen table explaining everyone's whereabouts. The place had the feel about it as if people had left hurriedly or unexpectedly. I brushed this impression off and thought Garry had decided to take the children out for hamburgers and fries. We usually eat at five and they would have been back by six. Rather than worry, I decided to try to enjoy the peace and quiet. I went into our bedroom to make the bed when the phone rang. It was Garry.

He started with some pleasantries: "Hi, how are you? How was your drive?" I gave him brief answers, all the time thinking "What is going on?" Then Garry said, "I am here at the emergency room at the hospital. Ben has a broken arm and they are taking him to surgery." I rushed to the hospital fearing that Ben might have some permanent damage to his arm.

It was not long until we were able to speak to the orthopedic specialist. Ben had broken both bones in his arm, at a point several inches above the wrist. The procedure they did is called a closed reduction because they did not have to open the skin at all to set the bones. Setting the two bones without anesthesia would have been an extremely painful process, and no one would have expected Ben to be able to lie quietly while the doctor did it. I was glad the emergency room doctor had called in a bone specialist to work on this bad break. He cast it from the wrist up over the elbow. The specialist told us it would probably take at least eight weeks to heal, but there would be no permanent damage. This was a relief! (See the picture of Ben with the cast on his arm seated with our favorite baby sitter, the one who had the oven scare.)

The accident occurred in a neighbor's yard, while Ben and his friend were playing on a ladder. Ben's playmate had climbed off the ladder and had gone into the house. Ben decided to do an experiment with the ladder -- attempting to use it as a pair of stilts! Despite what we have seen in old comedy movies, ladders do not make very good stilts. When the ladder fell, Ben's forearm was probably caught on the wrong side of a rung as it hit the ground.

That night I stayed in the hospital, sleeping when I could, on a couch in a waiting room just outside Ben's room. Several times during the night he woke up crying. I would go into the room, rub his forehead and cheeks until he fell back to sleep. The next morning a policeman came into Ben's room. He was very cheerful and pleasant. I thought "Isn't it wonderful of this off-duty officer to come to visit the children's unit of the hospital? Young children idealize anyone in uniform; What a thoughtful thing to do." It only occurred to me later that this was no off-duty officer, but someone performing an investigation! After all, this was Ben's third serious injury in an eighteen month period. One would not expect a child to have that many "accidents" in such a brief period of time.

The police officer did not stay in the room long. I was totally naive about why he was there and left the room shortly afterwards to go downstairs for breakfast. The officer went back into the room to question Ben after I had left. Many years later, when Ben and I were talking about his broken arm, he told me the officer wanted to know how things were at home: were we good to him, did we fight a lot, etc.

I am not offended in the least by the investigation. At the time, I had not known it occurred and when I found out I thought it was amusing. I asked Ben what his reaction was, as a six year old, to talking with the officer. He said, "I knew what he was doing. I was not about to tell him anything about our family."

After Ben's death, as I was talking with his therapist, she reminded me about those high-risk behaviors Ben had as a little boy. She said the fact he made it to fourteen was, in many respects, a tribute to the care we had given him. This helped me to put things a bit in perspective. Another thing that helped to give some perspective was to compare Ben's history of injuries with that of my childhood family. I grew up on a farm with seven siblings. Because of the machinery and large animals, farms can be very dangerous places. To hear that a farmer lost an arm or even his life in an accident is not uncommon. Yet all eight of us children managed to work on the farm and never break a single bone. If you multiply eight children by a minimum of 18 years you get a total of 1,728 months without a broken bone. Compare this with Ben. Here was a boy who had two broken bones and a concussion within eighteen months!

Ben's preschool years were difficult for me, but there was one aspect that was a real godsend. While I worked each day, Ben was cared for by a fantastic elderly couple, Mr. and Mrs. Backstrom. (Ben called them Grandma and Ray. See his picture with them) Their attachment to him was symbolized by the nickname they gave him: "Peanuts Backstrom." I could not have asked for a better child care situation for this overly sensitive, yet warm and loving child. Their house was as much a home to him as was ours. They had more time and patience to give to him than I did. They would play games with him, set up their camper in the back yard as a playhouse for him, and generally treat him like a cherished grandchild. Ben, in turn, adored them. No child was more fortunate in his day care than Ben.

With all the loving attention Ben was getting at the Backstrom's house, I did not feel motivated to send him to preschool. But as kindergarten approached, I decided to send him to a nursery school for part of the year to help him with the transition. There was a program three mornings a week not far from our home.

Ben was a little hesitant in his interaction with the kids at nursery school, but I did not see anything particularly unusual. At the end of the school year, the teacher met with the parents for a conference. She told us Ben was neither strong nor weak in any area. He was a typical kid and ready to start kindergarten next fall. But it was Ben who made an astute observation about himself.

There was a little four-year-old girl who came to "Grandma's" a few mornings a week. She was able to do a lot of things Ben was not able to do. For example, she was beginning to learn how to read, and it was coming easily and naturally for her. Ben wondered how it was possible for a child one year younger than himself to do things that he could not do. His life experience thus far had taught him that the older you were, the more you could do. Since this little girl was younger, her more grownup reading skills did not make sense to him. It was the first of many experiences in which other children were able to do things he could not do.

The summer after nursery school, Ben began having a problem with bedwetting. Toilet training had gone fairly well for him; at 24 months he had insisted on using the toilet. Grandma Backstrom called me to report how Ben had cried that day, insisting on using the toilet. She said he acted as if he knew what the toilet was for and suggested we give toilet training a try. Ben did use the toilet, but he also frequently wet his pants. We discontinued the training after a few weeks, thinking we should wait until Ben was a little more mature.

In August, when he was two-and-a-half, I tried again to toilet train Ben using praise and rewards, but got the same results: he willingly used the toilet, but wet his pants often. Since this method had not worked, another option was to use a different approach. I told the summer baby sitter that we would probably have to punish Ben for wetting. This is the opposite of what I had used to train Caroline. Praise and reward for using the toilet were effective for her, but with Ben the reverse seemed necessary. Rather than needing to learn when to use the toilet, he needed to learn when not to wet. This discipline actually worked very quickly for Ben, whereas praise and reward had been getting us nowhere. I recall Caroline telling me she thought the sitter was mean when she had Ben stand in the corner for wetting, but Ben was both day and night trained with this system within a week.

Early in June, when Ben was five years old, he suddenly started wetting the bed each night. Ben had wet the bed occasionally during the three years since being trained, but never like this. I assumed he had a bladder infection, but the urine sample I took into the doctor's office was negative. Ben drank a lot and urinated often, so my second guess was diabetes. The doctor's tests for that were also negative. Our physician suggested a one month trial of imipramine an anti-depressant with a side effect of urine retention.

The month-long trial of the imipramine did not significantly reduce his wetting, and we were then referred to a urologist. The doctor examined Ben and scheduled him for a kidney x-ray. The general findings were negative. Surgery could have been tried, but we were told it had only limited probability of solving the problem. Concerned about the possible terrifying effect surgery might have on a small boy, and the low probability of helping the wetting, we felt it did not seem worth the risk.

Ben continued to have some bedwetting throughout childhood, which probably hurt his self-esteem. None of our efforts improved the situation: decreasing liquids before bedtime, trial elimination of specific foods from his diet to test for allergies, waking him in the middle of the night to go to the bathroom, commercial devices to awaken him when he wet, or behavior modification. Finally, we simply put a plastic cover on his mattress, and got used to doing a lot of laundry. We also tried not to make a fuss about the wet sheets in the morning when they occurred.

It may seem paradoxical that this little boy, who later would be diagnosed as having depressive conditions, did not respond with complete success to antidepressants when given them at age six for bedwetting. Unfortunately, depressed children do not always do well with tricyclics such as imipramine. Also, the level prescribed for bedwetting is not a therapeutic dosage for depression. So although he had a problem with depression and was being treated with an antidepressant, the medication at that dosage was unfortunately ineffective for either the bedwetting or the depressive mood.

Bedwetting is another symptom associated with depression and anxiety in children. I now feel strongly that Ben's first major depressive episode may be dated as beginning on June 5, 1980, when his nightly bedwetting started. Although Ben was chronically depressed, I feel his first major mood swing may have occurred that June.

Early School Years

W hich of Ben's school problems were caused by his depression, which were related to his anxiety disorder, and which were due to his attention deficit hyperactive disorder? Separating them out is a big order, because some of the symptoms overlap. Here I will emphasize the symptoms that may be more related to his depression during his early elementary years, but ADHD will of necessity be included.

Ben's first year in school went all right. His teacher felt the kindergarten year should be exclusively devoted to social adjustment. She wanted children to be comfortable about coming to school. There was little pressure to perform, which made his kindergarten year a pleasant one for both Ben and me. At the end of the year, I went to the conference with the teacher. She explained that although she could not put her finger on it, she felt Ben might have some difficulty with school. How right she was!

INABILITY TO CONCENTRATE, SPEECH PECULIARITIES

In first grade, Ben had an excellent teacher who felt that reading was what first grade was all about. Unfortunately, Ben was turning out to be a weak reader. His biggest problems in school were his difficulty attending to tasks and getting his work done. His teacher began sending home his unfinished work and I began what became an ongoing process of making sure Ben completed his assignments.

At the end of first grade, his teacher and I agreed the best thing for him was to forget about school for the summer and concentrate on the things he wanted to do, such as swim and ride his bike. Garry and I felt this was especially important since his broken arm the previous summer had made those activities impossible. We decided to hope for the best, and perhaps by next fall he would be a little more mature.

Ben continued to have difficulty paying attention and completing assignments in second grade. At conference time in November, we discussed his problems with Ben's teacher. She thought Ben's problems were medical, and suggested he see a physician.

I took Ben to a pediatrician who had experience with children who had learning problems. The doctor recommended a three-day evaluation at a comprehensive clinic but suggested we wait until Ben was in third grade. The doctor found that the diagnostic team could be more accurate when the child was nine years old rather than only seven or eight. He could schedule Ben for the evaluation the next year.

I had observed something wrong with the way Ben talked. His articulation was fine, but his sentence structure was faulty. When he spoke, some of the words of the sentence were out of order. I requested a speech evaluation be done at Ben's school. The therapist met with me first to discuss my concerns. During our conversation, I mentioned our plans for the three day evaluations at a comprehensive clinic during third grade. The speech therapist shared her experience with medical evaluation of children with school problems. Often the finding is that there is nothing medically wrong with the child. Some parents are relieved to hear this, while others are upset that money had been spent on the evaluation and the child's school problem continues without any help toward a solution. She suggested we consider requesting an evaluation by the learning disabilities (LD) teacher there at the school. This would be done at no cost to us.   Her suggestion made a lot of sense.

The results of the speech evaluation showed that Ben's speech was all right, and his vocabulary was within normal limits. I realize now that what I observed in Ben's speech is part of what psychiatrist Dr. Charles Popper described as "cognitive looseness."

COGNITIVE LOOSENESS

According to Dr. Popper, children with either attention deficit hyperactive disorder or bipolar illness have speech that is hard for the listener to follow. These children "can give disorganized narratives and make logical leaps that are non-psychotic but still hard to follow."   For example, when Ben described what happened in a TV program, the story he told was not in consecutive order. It would be extremely difficult for the listener to figure out what actually happened on the TV program.

This "cognitive looseness" would naturally cause problems in reading comprehension. When a child can not even clearly describe what happens in a story he has both heard and seen on TV, it is easy to understand the difficulty he would have in making sense of a story he had read. Further, if the child does not comprehend what he is reading, there is little logic or pleasure in reading at all. Such kids, obviously, are not motivated to read. Depressed kids are often described as unmotivated. Little wonder!

During third grade Ben continued to struggle with his work and I continued to help him with it. One of the assignments each week was for him to write a story. The teacher would help the children get the story started by giving them the first three or four sentences. (Coincidentally, I had used this same technique when I taught elementary school and found it enormously successful.) Since Ben had difficulty functioning on his own, he often brought home this assignment with very little completed. We would re-read the beginning sentences and discuss various possibilities of how to finish the story. In these assignments, I again saw examples of the "cognitive looseness," -- disorganized narrative which made "logical leaps that are not psychotic but still hard to follow." In Ben's writing, I saw the written form of this cognitive looseness. His narratives were jumbled; they did not make sense.

OPPOSITIONAL BEHAVIOR

The diagnostic category "oppositional" behaviors is controversial among child and adolescent therapists. It describes a youngster who, as the term implies, does not do what parents, teachers, and other adults ask him or her to do. Some mental health professionals question whether there really is a disorder such as this, or if the child's unwillingness to comply is a natural outgrowth of being asked to do things that are difficult. No one who knew Ben would have said he was abrasively defiant, but anyone who tried long and hard to help him get his daily work done would have experienced a form of this problem.

The official diagnosis of oppositional behaviors have gone through an evolution during the last years. According to the DSM -IV, oppositional defiant disorder occurs when :

A. A pattern of negativistic, hostile, and defiant behavior lasting at least 6 months, during which four (or more) of the following are present:

1. often losing temper;
2. often arguing with adults;
3. often actively defies or refuses to comply with adults'
    requests;
4. often deliberately annoying people;
5. often blaming others for his or her mistakes or misbehavior
6. often being touchy or easily annoyed by others;
7. often being angry and resentful;
8. often being spiteful or vindictive;

B.   The disturbance in behavior causes clinically significant impairment in social, academic, or occupational functioning.

Like every problem Ben had, the symptoms showed themselves gradually.   During the summer following second grade, rather than send him to summer school to catch up, I had him do some very short review math sheets at home. Ben's reaction was to complain often and try to negotiate a reduction of the assignment. Ben wanted both to achieve and to be excused from doing the work it required. Often during his elementary years, when things would not go well for him, Ben would tell me we were not strict enough. It was as if he did not have enough internal structure or discipline to control himself, so he wanted something from the outer world to impose restrictions and control over him. He knew the other kids were able to handle school and other life situations. He saw that the parents of his friends expected a lot from their children and were firm. He wanted to succeed and wanted us to be strict enough to produce this result. The paradox is that when I would attempt to organize his time by giving him constructive activities, he would spend a great amount of energy trying to get out of doing them.

Sometimes the structures I would set up would be developed by both of us sitting down and negotiating a plan. One example of this was the amount of TV he could watch; the number of hours spent on school work would equal the number of hours in which he was allowed to watch TV. Plans like that worked out fairly well for him. Ben, like many depressed kids, could spend excessive amounts of time watching TV rather than engaging in social or sports activities. Setting some limits to TV watching by making it contingent on the child's activity was helpful.

As Ben got older, I would sometimes tell him about all the work I had to do when I was his age. Ben would say, "Mother, you're you. You can do that stuff. I'm me. I'm different." And of course he was right. If Ben had not had an attention deficit disorder and a depressive illness, he would have been able to do what I wanted him to do, what his teachers wanted him to do, and what he probably wanted to do. But when something is wrong with a child, some of these goals may not be possible.

ILLNESSES DURING EARLY ELEMENTARY SCHOOL

Ben's childhood was plagued with frequent illnesses. I am not sure how much of this illness can be attributed to depression and how much of it might have been allergies, but I know Ben had many more colds, flu, stomach aches, headaches, and ear infections than most kids. If there was anything to catch during the school year, Ben caught it. My husband and I wrestled over whether to make Ben go to school when he was not feeling well or to keep him home. If he stayed home every time he was not feeling well, he would miss a great deal of school. We did not want him to have even more problems because of absences; he would also have a lot of makeup work to complete when he finally did return. Further, since Ben did not seem to like school, we feared he would use sickness as a way out.

Often when we sent him to school he would feel fine, but other times he would feel miserable all day long. Occasionally, the teacher noticed Ben's inattentiveness, and sent him to the nurse's office. We finally discovered a solution which allowed him to stay home but did not reinforce being sick; it also encouraged him to make good use of his time. He was not to watch TV, and he had to be in bed where he could sleep, read, draw, or use his educational toys. I called his teacher in the morning and asked her to send home Ben's assignments. I would either pick them up myself or a neighborhood boy would bring them to our house. Ben did the assignment that afternoon and evening so was not behind in his work.

I do not think Ben's illnesses were fabricated. His temperature was real, the cough and congestion were real, the pain in his head or ears was real, and the vomit was real. I can not be certain whether the cause of his physical illness was his depression (because depression does affect one's immune system), if Ben had allergies which may have caused some of these symptoms, or if the illnesses were caused by a combination of depression and possible allergies. I only know the situation was uncomfortable for everyone.

After lots of problems with colds and congestion, Ben developed a hearing problem. An ear specialist recommended tubes be put in; this necessitated day surgery.

ATTEMPT TO GET A DIAGNOSIS / MISUNDERSTOOD BY OTHERS

When fourth grade began, I continued to help Ben every evening with his homework. Ben was making a lot of errors when he did his assignments. I wanted him to have some success with his work and to learn to work carefully. To help him with this problem, I would check his assignments after he had done them, and erase all the incorrect answers. I would have him re-do those items that were wrong.

I worked with Ben to produce correct assignments for two reasons. First, since doing schoolwork was so torturous for him, I did not want him to go through the process of actually finishing the work only to receive an F because of the errors. I wanted him to have some chance of getting reinforcement and have a reason to keep trying. If his errors were found and corrected, his odds of doing acceptable work would improve.

Second, I wanted to reinforce the value of doing the work carefully and correctly the first time. The fewer errors he made, the fewer he would have to re-do.

But this process of identifying errors and correcting them made Ben angry. He felt he had gotten the work done and now I was insisting that he re-do part of it. I do not know if this was part of an oppositional defiant disorder or just a typical reaction.

I thought Ben had a learning problem, and I wanted him to get services in the school so he could do some work there. As fourth grade began, I went ahead with the request for an evaluation by the learning disabilities (L.D.) teacher.

Ben's aptitude (what he is capable of doing) was compared to his achievement (what his actual performance was) in those subjects. His aptitude was approximately one year higher than his achievement in both reading and math. The findings of the evaluation meant he did not meet the eligibility requirement for services as learning disabled. With no help from school forthcoming, I looked into the possibility of getting someone else to help him with homework. I contacted a former elementary teacher and asked him to work with Ben each day after school. Arrangements were made for Ben to catch the city bus after school and go to his tutor's home for approximately two hours of help. He would then catch a bus home. Ben went to this tutor for several months and later, when the teacher was unable to continue doing the work, I hired an older student to take over the tutoring for the last few months of the year.

ANGER AND IRRITABILITY

During the spring of Ben's fourth grade year I became influenced by the work of Elisabeth Kubler-Ross. She is most well-known for her work on death and dying, but I heard her give a talk at a conference for persons interested in children with learning problems. She spoke on the importance of communicating to children that your love for them is not based on their behavior or their work performance. Specifically, she advised parents to hug their children at least once every day and tell them they are special, a gift from God; you will always love them no matter what.

Children's television personality, Mr. Rogers, conveys much the same message. He often says things like: "I like having you in my neighborhood because you are special," "I like you because you are you," and "I like you just the way you are." When my children were younger and watched his show, I often wondered whether Mr. Rogers made this statement at the close of each program because it was the one thing he wanted them to remember most of all.

After hearing Dr. Kubler-Ross's powerful lecture, it was clear to me that I had been right to change my focus to giving Ben reassurance rather than help with his homework. I decided to concentrate on giving him unconditional love while he received help with his homework from someone else. I am glad I took this approach. For about two years I made sure I hugged Ben at least two or three times a day and told him he was special, a gift from God, and I would always love him no matter what. After a time I found he seemed less angry. Shortly before he died, Ben told me that of all the things we did to help with his depression, the one thing that seemed to work best were the hugs and statements of unconditional love. This is why I feel so strongly that emotional support is essential in any program for students.

I remember a Mother's Day card he wrote. It told me he would always love me no matter what. Right now the memory of this card is very precious to me.

Upper Elementary Years

FIFTH GRADE

When Ben entered fifth grade, he had two teachers: a morning teacher and an afternoon one. Ben liked both of his teachers very much and his promotion to upper elementary school was uplifting to him. He wanted to perform well for these teachers, but his difficulty getting his work done, legibly and on time, continued.

My husband, Garry, decided this would be the year he would volunteer to take over the nightly homework supervision. The first half of the school year seemed to go well, but during the second semester I would often hear Ben crying in his room late at night. One night when I went in to comfort him; he said that he wanted so much to do well in school, but he always seemed to do poorly. He wanted so much to get A's and B's on his own, but no matter what he did or how hard he tried, unless he got help he always got D's or F's.

In the past, when we had attended parent/teacher conferences, Ben's difficulties were often described as problems with work habits and motivation. As I sat there listening to Ben I thought, "Do children with motivational problems cry in their beds at night because they aren't doing well in school?" It did not make sense to me. I told Ben I knew he sincerely wanted to do well, and I was going to find a way to help him. Ben's response was, "You have no idea what it means to me to have someone who understands."

I went to the next scheduled meeting of an association of parents who have children with learning disabilities. One of their pamphlets described some of the symptoms which included:

1. short attention span (restless, easily distracted)
2. reverses letters and numbers
3. personal disorganization (can not follow simple
        schedules)
4. impulsive and inappropriate behavior (poor
        judgment in social situations, talks and acts
        before thinking)
5. inconsistent performance (can not remember today
        what was learned yesterday)
6. speech problems (immature speech development,
        has trouble expressing ideas)

All of this sounded like Ben to me!

At the parent's meeting, I found out there was going to be a conference the following month on learning disabilities. I decided to attend. I also decided to find out what other resources were available in our city for children with learning problems. I contacted the Human Development Center to find out if they had any suggestions regarding tutors. A therapist told me that the Language Therapy Center in our town evaluated children and then referred them to a tutor who is trained in the Orton Gillingham method, a system used for young people with dyslexia (reading, spelling, and writing problems).

My attempts to get someone to recognize the true nature of Ben's problem led me to attend the conference on learning disabilities in April of 1986. It was there I learned that dyslexia is a problem of brain anatomy, while attention deficit disorder may be more a problem with brain chemistry as it relates to the functioning of specific parts of the brain. I also learned that some young people with learning disabilities commit suicide, especially when depression occurs along with the learning disability. The speaker mentioned that a small dose of antidepressant medication is often helpful to patients with ADHD.

Later the same month, I scheduled Ben for an appointment at the Language Therapy Center in our city. In the therapist's opinion, Ben had a mild form of dyslexia. Specialized tutoring was recommended. The minimum length of the program was two years with the student meeting with the therapist three hours per week for one-hour sessions. A trained tutor lived fairly close to our home, and Ben began lessons soon afterwards.

Some of the evaluator's observations of Ben were insightful. She wrote:

> Ben was cooperative and friendly during the entire period. He took the initiative, beginning and completing all requested tasks promptly. He was verbally facile. His conversation was at a much more mature level than his written work. He seemed much older than 11 years old. He was quick and accurate on lots of the testing. When things became difficult on the spelling and writing tasks, his errors became more evident. He tried to please, however.

Looking back on her comments, I find them to be an accurate description of Ben when his depression was not particularly acute. Her comment on his maturity was especially important. Most adults, when meeting Ben for the first time, got the impression Ben was precocious, not disabled. I often wonder if this was not part of the reason Ben never was able to get the academic help he needed; he did not seem to need it.

At the conference at the end of fifth grade, I met with both teachers to share my conviction that Ben had a learning problem, not just a motivation problem. One of these men had spent some time as a teacher of exceptionally bright children. Now as a teacher of a regular fifth grade students, he challenged his students by giving them at least one discussion question each class period designed to really make them think. He would stretch the minds of the average students while giving the bright students a challenge. His comment about Ben was intriguing. He said, "If that boy could ever get his act together about doing his work, he could really go places. Quite often he gives the most astute, insightful answers of any student in the class." To me, this again pointed to Ben's maturity as well as the potential buried under the combination of attention deficit, depression, and anxiety disorder.

At this conference, I mentioned that Ben was evaluated and would likely receive services from the Language Therapy Center. I also requested a re-evaluation for learning disability services from the school system. Ben was again evaluated by the LD teacher in May of 1986. At the end of the month, we met with the LD teacher, the school psychologist, one of his fifth-grade teachers, a sixth grade teacher he would have the following September, and the principal. Her findings from individualized testing were essentially the same as they had been early in fourth grade: Ben did not qualify for services.

The whole process of attempting to obtain help for my child was very painful. Most other students did twice as well as my son did with less effort. The unfairness of the situation was discouraging for all of us. I understand why many young people just give up trying.

In my frustration that spring, I went through the lecture notes I had taken during the learning disabilities' conference. Once again I was impressed by the work quality of the neurologist, Dr. Drake Dune from the Mayo Clinic, in Rochester, Minnesota. It occurred to me to take Ben to the Mayo Clinic for an evaluation. The clinic was only a five hour drive from our home. The question still remained in my mind: was Ben's problem a matter of work habits and motivation, or did he, in fact, have a learning disability? If we could not get a definitive answer to the question at the Mayo Clinic, I felt we probably could not get an answer any place else either.

When I had comforted Ben as he cried that night about his problems with school, I told him I felt his problems were not his fault, but resulted from some sort of learning problem. I told him I was determined to find out what it was and to get him the necessary help. A few days after our conversation, Ben emerged from his bedroom where he was attempting to do his school work, and said to me, "Maybe my problem is that I am just plain lazy." I smiled at him and thought, "How many adults have the psychological honesty to take a good hard look at themselves and conclude that some of their problem is of their own making?" My respect for my son grew that day. It is true that Ben was not the most ambitious child, but this is also true of many other children who do just fine in school. It is hard to know what role the depression had in Ben's inability to stay concentrated or to do his work, and what role the attention deficit played. The inability to concentrate is a classic symptom of both conditions.

Ben was given an appointment at Mayo for the following September, several months away. In the meantime, I wondered if we could start the small dosage of the antidepressant mentioned in the lecture by the Mayo neurologist as being helpful to some children with attention deficit. The medication sometimes helps with the sleep disturbance and thus improves alertness the next day. Ben had reported having a great deal of trouble getting to sleep and feeling tired the next day at school. I hoped the medication would help him.

I took Ben to a local psychiatrist in hopes he would see the benefits of starting him on an antidepressant medication. The psychiatrist noted in his report that Ben had been referred because of problems with insomnia. Ben told him he was sick often and had frequent headaches. The psychiatrist noted that Ben had unreasonable feelings of guilt about many aspects of his life. Ben shared with the doctor his pervasive fear of "being goaded into some kind of excessive action" when with peers. This last symptom may reflect Ben's impulsivity, another common symptom of both attention deficit and bipolar illness. The psychiatrist decided not to prescribe the antidepressant, recommending instead we wait for the Mayo evaluation in September.

Summer came and Ben started the specialized tutoring. Besides this, I thought about the suggestion made during the conference on learning disabilities -- to accentuate skills and talents the individual possessed rather than concentrating only on areas in which the child had difficulty. Since Ben had a strong interest in computers and seemed to have some talent in that area, I registered Ben in a keyboarding class at summer school. We purchased a computer that summer, and Ben began to work with it.

SIXTH GRADE

In September, Ben had his appointment at the Mayo Clinic. It was a three day evaluation and covered everything: blood work, hearing and vision testing, an electrocardiogram and an electroencephalogram, speech and educational testing, appointments with a psychologist and a psychiatrist, and an interview with the neurologist -- the expert of learning disability I heard lecture in spring. Ben enjoyed his adventure at Mayo. He thought of Mayo as the Disney World of Medicine. He liked their high-tech, yet friendly, approach.

During the appointment with the neurologist, Ben spoke alone with him for about thirty minutes; then I was called in to join them. The doctor felt Ben did not have dyslexia because his reading in this one-on-one setting was not that far below grade level. Ben's performance in reading seemed more characterized by a hesitancy or unwillingness to do it, rather than an inability to read. He also wondered why Ben was so mature. Ben was 11 1/2 at the time, and the neurologist said that Ben's manner and conversation was more mature than he usually sees from 14 or 15 year olds. (This had been the same impression the other evaluator had of Ben.)

At the end of the three days, I attended the summary conference where the results of all the testing were presented. The team recommendations were made at this time. There were three significant observations: First, Ben's verbal IQ was at the 77th percentile, while his performance IQ was at the 37th percentile. This meant verbally he was above average, but he performed below average. Second, Ben had a noticeable emotional dysfunction. Third, he had a mild but significant difficulty with attention.

They recommended Ben begin an antidepressant medication for the attention deficit; he should be considered for LD services at school in the areas of spelling and written language; and he should see a psychiatrist on an outpatient basis for at least a trial period. When presented with these recommendations, Ben was vehement about not wanting to see a psychiatrist. He felt seeing a psychiatrist would label him as different and defective. Also, he had been upset by his experience with a psychiatrist the previous spring and did not wish to see this doctor again.

I assured Ben that no one was going to push him into something against his will. At that time, our community did not include a psychiatrist who specialized in adolescents. Going to a larger city for appointments would require a six or seven hour round trip each time. I would have to do some research about whom he should see, and that would take time.

When the November teacher's conferences were set up, we wrote a note to his teachers letting them know we would share the Mayo report with them. At the meeting, we met with one of his teachers who showed interest in the report. His other teacher did not attend the conference and later called us complaining that Ben was doing some of his school work on the computer rather than writing it out by hand. She felt allowing him to turn in typewritten work would be treating him differently from the other children, a practice of which she did not approve.

The next month we had a meeting with the principal and both of Ben's teachers. This is the first conference in which I felt the system was listening to us rather than talking at us. I mentioned the importance of Ben seeing some hope and not despairing. There had been several suicides at our local high school that year, and I mentioned what the neurologist had said about young people with learning disabilities and depression being at risk. At this conference the school agreed to accept some of his homework done on the computer. It was also decided not to grade Ben at all on handwriting. The remaining time in sixth grade seemed to go fairly smoothly. Ben was receiving private tutoring in reading skills, Garry was helping him study for tests at school, and I was continuing to provide emotional support.

Seventh Grade

H ow would Ben cope with junior high? He was always a totally disorganized child. How was he going to cope with 6 different classrooms and 6 different teachers? Ben's elementary teachers might have been frustrated in their attempt to work with him, but they at least became accustomed to his problems. They were with him all day and came to realize that Ben was basically a nice boy for whom school was a struggle. Would his junior high teachers just view him as a non-compliant student?

Then there were the challenges from peers. Ben was overly sensitive and lacked social skills; thus he felt uncomfortable with other young people. How was he going to cope with so many unfamiliar fellow students? Additionally, it is typical for 9th graders to harass the incoming 7th graders. What would the hazing process be like for him during this first year? Peer pressure becomes a major issue as students enter the teen years. Since Ben had very limited impulse control, he was especially vulnerable to being led into problem behaviors. What kind of trouble was this thirteen, fourteen, and fifteen year old going to get into in junior high?

When a young person has problems learning in school, the gap between what he can do and what other students his age can widens each year. Would this cause him to view himself as neither one of the "good" students who excel nor one of the "regular guys?" Would he become one of the lower rung of the junior high social class? I was concerned about what low self-esteem would produce in this energized teenager. All of this worried me.

All through sixth grade, we were paying for the services of a private tutor. Ben's work on reading skills had begun positively, but lately he had seemed to be resistant to instruction. The oppositional defiance, so common with bipolar children, was making itself evident. Ben often worked against the people who were trying to help him. I saw this very clearly when I helped him with his homework. The tutor decided Ben needed a break from her instruction. I took a look at what I could do to help prepare Ben for seventh grade.

My daughter, Caroline, had been in that same school four years earlier, so I had some clues about what Ben would face. I knew he would be taking a health class in which he would write three research papers. For Ben, this would be an overwhelming task. Failure to do these papers at all, or doing them poorly, would be especially unfortunate for Ben because he was genuinely interested in the functions of the body, health, and healing. When Garry had his gallbladder surgery, it was Ben who showed more interest in the surgery than anyone else. He had many questions for the surgeon, who in turn showed an interest in him.

I did not want Ben to have a discouraging experience in health. Further, since I had heard so many positive things about the class from Caroline, I wanted Ben to have a good experience as well. I also wanted to continue his use of the computer as an aid to doing acceptable looking school work, so I hit upon the idea of having him work on these three papers during the summer. He could have three months to learn how to do a research paper; he would use the computer, and he would learn to find his numerous errors and correct them without erasures and mess. Ben would do actual assignments he could hand in during the upcoming year! I hoped he would feel he had a head start for 7th grade and feel more prepared for what he was to face. I hoped it would improve his self-confidence.

While working on the papers, his old problem with cognitive looseness was painfully evident. The disorganized narrative and the tendency to make illogical leaps made his ideas hard to follow. I spent a lot of time working on the papers with Ben to help him produce something that made sense and gave him some help in how to spot his errors. These papers were a big project for Ben and me. We were both frustrated by the time we finished the last of the three papers at the end of August.

The research papers were our effort to improve Ben's reading and writing skills. To address my other concern, that of Ben handling himself with older peers, we looked at Aikido, one of the martial arts. We chose it because of the principle of this form of self-defense. Its aim is the neutralization of an attacker, rather than aggression. The goal of Aikido is not to hurt someone else but to disarm and escape attack. Aikido is suited to all ages and body types, so it would be ideal to help a smaller student to defend himself against a larger one.

I felt it was important for Ben to learn a non-violent, non-aggressive means of coping with possible harassment or intimidation from the ninth graders who were bigger and stronger. I hoped the Aikido training might also help him feel more confident about handling whatever situation arose. The classes were available at the local YMCA. Ben took lessons that summer and enjoyed this mental and physical training program.

(Recently I learned that martial arts are an especially good sport for students with ADHD.)

When seventh grade approached, I held my breath and crossed my fingers. It turned out to be a pleasant surprise. Much of seventh grade went well for Ben. He was taking a low dosage of imipramine at bedtime, which seemed to help him sleep and feel more alert the next day. He arose each morning with his alarm clock, showered, got his own breakfast and caught the 7:10 bus. This was quite a switch for us. All six years of elementary school we had to coax him out of bed, get out the clothes he was to wear, make his breakfast for him, and drive him to school at 8:45. Ben in seventh grade was like a different kid.

He liked all his teachers, but he especially admired his math teacher. Although math was a struggle for him, he felt comfortable in the structured environment this teacher established in his classroom. Band was another surprise for us. Getting him to practice was not the problem I thought it was going to be, because playing the trombone was one of Ben's talents. He had good things to say about all of his teachers.

He enjoyed his health class, and since his three research papers were already done, he could relax knowing things would turn out fairly well for him. Ben's health teacher gave each student a questionnaire to fill out that gave parents some insights into their children. The title on the top read: "These are some things about school and you and me." I think it gives some fairly revealing looks into Ben's thinking. A careful reading of his responses shows the social isolation he felt, his concern over his grades, and his need for us to understand his struggle.

1. The class I enjoy the most is <u>Band</u>, because <u>it's cool.</u>

2. The class I learn the most in is <u>Band</u>, because <u>it's cool</u>.

3. I have to work the hardest in <u>Math</u>, because <u>teacher</u>

4. People I like to or would like to spend time with in school are <u>me</u>.

5. This year, I hope I can or will <u>Pass 7 grade</u>

6. A goal of some kind <u>get good grades</u>

7. As my parents or guardians, you have helped me <u>Pick up my towels in my</u> room <u>(Ha) (ha)</u>

8. As my parents or guardians, I would like you to/or need from you, <u>your money, your car and your pitty.</u> (pity misspelled)

9. My feelings about you are <u>your prity</u> (pretty is misspelled and then crossed out and replaced by) <u>really cool</u>.

The fact that our son appreciated our efforts to help him gave us motivation to hang in there when the going got tough.

That year Ben developed an interest in ham radio and wanted us to buy him one. We hesitated. A ham radio is an expensive item, and I did not want to spend a lot of money for what might turn out to be a passing whim. After some thought, we made an agreement. Since we had to forego our yearly family vacation to Florida at Christmas time because of a special event for our daughter, we would give Ben the money we would have spent on an airplane ticket for him had we gone. He would have the first half of what was needed to buy the radio. If he was still serious about buying the radio when next Christmas rolled around, we would give him the other half of the money. I gave the money to him in $1 bills along with a lock box to keep it in. I thought saving the money in that form would be a good discipline for him. He liked the arrangement and he was very careful with the money.

Seventh grade was also the year Ben began to see a pediatric cardiologist. At his Mayo Clinic evaluation in sixth grade, the doctors had found Ben's cholesterol level was 223. Since 200 is the upper limits of what can still be considered within the normal range for an adult, Ben's level was considered extremely high cholesterol for a boy his age. Re-testing at age twelve showed Ben's level was 240. The pediatrician suggested he see the pediatric cardiologist who came to our town bimonthly. The specialist recommended Ben increase his exercise, decrease the fat content of his diet, and try to lose some weight.

Throughout Ben's childhood, I had tried a number of methods to help him do precisely that. He would lose weight for a time, but as with most people who "battle the bulge," he would quickly regain any losses. Since my husband also had elevated cholesterol, we decided this time we would begin a family campaign to change eating patterns. The emphasis was not on weight but on the reduction of both Garry's and Ben's cholesterol.

One of my sisters had died of heart failure at the age of thirteen, so I knew it is possible for a young person to have a serious cardiac condition requiring careful treatment. There was also a history of heart disease in Garry's family. We took Ben's 240 cholesterol level seriously. That winter and the early spring of Ben's seventh grade, he lost 13 pounds and his cholesterol dropped 40 points.

The very last weeks of school, Ben began doing something he had never done before: he started going to the neighborhood park with friends. I felt uncomfortable about what he was doing there, and although I was glad to see him interacting with other young people, I did not get the impression they were doing positive things. With summertime coming up, I began to wonder what kind of trouble Ben might get into during his idle hours.

What positive activities might he have to occupy himself? His grades had been good enough in his first year of junior high, so we felt he deserved some reinforcement by getting a break from school work. But he needed something to occupy his time. We decided to emphasize other types of work. Ben agreed to do some work at home and for our group home business. He would do some lawn mowing, painting, and house cleaning.

What a relief it was coming home to a house cleaned by my son rather than messed up by him! The house did not get as messy when Ben, who created the lion's share of the messes, realized it would be part of his job to clean it up. The painting and lawn mowing he did at our group home was as good as many of our other employees had done.

But Ben's work schedule did not keep Ben from getting into mischief. I remember one summer day when something he said gave me a clue. I had asked him how things were going, and his response was, "I'm trying it all, Mother." I knew one of the things he was doing in the park with his friends was smoking, but I wondered if he was not also experimenting with other substances. There was an isolated incident with experimentation with alcohol but no evidence of any drug use. After Ben's death, I had some frank talks with his friends about this, and they were quite insistent that Ben had not been experimenting with drugs. So, to my knowledge, his "trying it all" may have consisted only of chewing and smoking tobacco and a single bout with alcohol.

In July, Garry and I attended a conference in Chicago. Garry went to the first week of the conference, and I attended the second week. We went at different times so we would only be gone from Ben for the weekend between the meetings. While in Chicago we contacted an old friend, a psychiatrist who is an expert in the diagnoses of depression. Our friend suggested that Ben's genetic background would make him a likely candidate to have bipolar (manic depressive) illness. I asked him for a treatment referral somewhere in our state. He told me to send him the report from Mayo and he would contact someone at University Hospital in Minneapolis.

After returning from Chicago, I told Ben we thought his depression was bipolar illness. I also mentioned my suspicions about his "trying it all" with his friends. The treatment for his illness would start as soon as the referral process was complete. Until then, we wanted to help Ben avoid any experimentation with street drugs and any other trouble he might be getting into. Specifically, I asked Ben to stop going to the park with his friends. He promised to try to do this but said he would need some help saying "No" to these kids. I volunteered to act as a "door guard" telling these kids either Ben was unavailable, or was busy working, or was not allowed out of the house. For the most part, I could be careful about the exact wording of what I told them and manage not to lie. But at that point I did not hesitate to do what was needed to break his connection with them. I had always taught my children to be helpful or kind to others when they came to the door, so my playing the heavy took some getting used to for all of us.

It was about this time that a new friend came into Ben's life. At first I was a little leery of Ben's new friendship, but it was not long before I began to hope this boy might be a true friend to him. He was two years older than Ben and an outdoors enthusiast. He shared Ben's interest in fishing and hunting, and he had a job at a nearby stable. One day Ben accompanied him to work where they did the chores together. Ben came home sore after spending four hours of shoveling out the stalls but said he had a great time. Ben decided he wanted a job at the stables more than anything else in the world. I advised him to do some volunteer work. He would learn a lot about the horses and the operation of the stables, and then when one of the other employees quit their job the owner would see the advantage of hiring Ben.

His first reaction was negative. Although he loved the work, not getting paid seemed unreasonable to him. Ben liked being with his friend; he loved being with the horses. He actually did not mind shoveling out the stalls, so in the end Ben volunteered at the stables quite often. The owner of the stables liked Ben and was friendly toward this unpaid worker.

During that summer, Ben learned a little Morse code in preparation for the ham radio. We had a tall aerial installed for Ben which could be used both for the ham, when he got it, and for the CB he had borrowed. Ben always enjoyed talking with adults and made quite a number of CB buddies.

We hoped we were keeping Ben occupied and out of trouble while waiting for treatment to begin, but towards the end of the summer Ben had the one incident with alcohol I mentioned earlier. One morning when we tried to get him up to mow a lawn, we discovered he was drunk. Later, we searched his room and found two pint bottles: one empty and one almost full. His words, "I'm trying it all, Mother" came back to me. Garry and I confronted him with what we had found. We wanted to know what was going on. "I'm a kid. I'm experimenting with things. Didn't you want to try things when you were young?" was his explanation.

I tried to get some perspective on his response. His comment made me think about my own drinking when I was young. For the last twenty years, my drinking had consisted of a glass of wine two or three times a year, but when I was younger I drank much more. My youthful drinking was associated with social events, and its purpose was to become less inhibited, thus allowing me to have more fun at parties and dances. The idea of Ben, at age thirteen, drinking alone in his room to the point of getting sick did not seem to be normal drinking behavior. It did not have anything at all to do with having fun. We had some more frank talks about his possible illness, and Ben told us he was at last willing to see a psychiatrist.

As summer drew to an end, I was encouraged that Ben had a new friend and was becoming involved in outdoor activities. I was impatient for the referral process to speed up so Ben could start seeing someone for further evaluation and treatment. I was concerned about his impulsive, experimental behaviors, and I was cognizant that we were running out of time with Ben. Up to this point, Ben had always been willing to cooperate with us. He would soon get into the age in which parental defiance is to be expected.

Eighth Grade

In September, some of the weight Ben lost the previous spring was still off. He had also grown a few inches during the summer and he did not look overweight. He felt good about his body image as school began. Depressed young people have a tendency to either overeat or not eat enough, and the food issue was a constant problem for Ben. He had marked fluctuations in his weight. In the middle of May, when Garry and he were conscientiously working to reduce cholesterol, Ben had gotten down to 152 pounds. By early November he was up to 178.

Some of that weight gain may have occurred during the summer when Ben was alone in the house and it was harder for us to monitor him. He had difficulty controlling his own eating without someone around to encourage him to eat properly. At Ben's first appointment with the psychiatrist in mid-October, he weighed 170. At his follow-up appointment, he was up to 178. Part of the eight pound gain in those three weeks may have been due to lithium. This medication, a natural element, is like salt, and is helpful to many people with bipolar illness. But it can also cause increased appetite. Unfortunately for Ben, he was caught between the complications of management of depressive illness and the management of his weight, a risk factor in cardiovascular problems.

Before his first appointment with the psychiatrist in October, Ben and I had a talk. He looked forward to telling the psychiatrist what was really going on in his life. This adolescent who had so vehemently refused to see anyone two years earlier was now serious about dealing with his problems. I was proud of him.

Ben's psychiatrist specializes in working with adolescents, and she was able to establish a rapport with him almost immediately. After talking with him alone, she asked us to join them. The plan was for Ben to see her every three weeks and for him to start medication. He could either start on an antidepressant only or the lithium only. Since Ben's genetic background indicated bipolar illness and lithium is the most important medication for the condition, it was agreed to start with the lithium and add the antidepressant later if needed.

At home, Garry and I continued to encourage Ben to occupy himself with activities that he enjoyed. Ben volunteered at the stables each weekend that autumn. He also showed enthusiasm for hunting. With the approach of hunting season, Ben needed to take a gun safety class if he was to go hunting with his friend, Garry, and Garry's friend. Ben signed up for a night class offered by community schools. He did some studying and managed to pass the gun safety tests.

Shooting a gun was another thing Ben was good at. He had started to do some trap shooting with my husband and seemed to have some talent for it. The end of the gun safety class coincided with the beginning of hunting season. The hunting foursome consisted of the two boys and two men. Something about the two older men sharing a hunting experience with the boys struck me as just the right kind of thing for the guys to do together.

Ben was seeing his therapist every three weeks. He genuinely liked her and felt these visits and the medication were helpful to him. In late November or early December the decision was made to add an antidepressant because Ben was still experiencing depression even with the lithium. What antidepressant should Ben use? Psychiatrists have found that if a particular medication or combination of medications work well for one member of a family, they often work well for other members of the family. This is logical since family members often have similar body chemistry, and they typically have similar reactions to medications. This is especially true with illnesses that have a strong genetic factor. My husband had been taking Prozac since January of 1988 and had been doing well with the combination of it and the lithium he had started late in August of that same year. Ben's biological make-up probably would be similar to Garry's, and since Prozac had worked well for Garry, it was a logical choice.

When talking about the Prozac, the subject of potential side effects was raised. Prozac did not have many of the side effects that other antidepressants like the tricyclics have. But Ben's psychiatrist did inform us that Prozac can trigger mania in persons with bipolar (manic-depressive) illness. Another temporary side effect for some people taking Prozac is weight loss. We were already familiar with this from the experience my husband had with the medication. Garry started taking Prozac soon after the medication came on the market, and he originally shed some of his unwanted weight. Garry still experienced problems with mood swings when taking Prozac alone. When he began taking the lithium he stabilized and so did his appetite. The lithium may have increased Garry's appetite, but we can not be sure.

Ben started with one capsule of Prozac a day and then went to two capsules daily after his next visit with the psychiatrist in mid December. Two capsules a day is the usual dosage for that medication. Shortly after starting the two Prozac a day, Ben became more impulsive.

I remember the psychiatrist saying Prozac can trigger manic behavior in some patients with bipolar illness. I called her on the phone saying, "I think we may have produced mania in this manic-depressive." I described what seemed to be some increased impulsive, unstable behaviors. She could not be certain the medication had actually caused heightened impulsivity. When one is dealing with an impulsive kid, it is very difficult to know exactly how to proceed. Medications which help raise depressed mood may also raise the type of behavior one is prone to display whenever you feel energetic. When Ben was depressed, he did not have much energy, but when less depressed, his energies would not necessarily channel themselves into orderly, constructive activity. With his ADHD compounding the bipolar illness, his impulsive behaviors had the potential for being challenging for both him and us.

The psychiatrist did not suggest any change in medication, but instead recommended Ben begin to see a therapist in our own town while continuing to see her for the monitoring of the medicine. Since our city did not have a psychiatrist who specializes in child or adolescent mental illness, I did not know whom I could take Ben to see, but I took her suggestion under consideration.

In January, I did take Ben to a local psychiatrist. During the interview, Ben and I gave her some background information about his problem and what we had been doing about it. The woman seemed genuinely willing to help us, but in the car on the way home Ben made it very clear he was not interested at all in being in therapy with her. Since he showed such resistance to the efforts of the local therapist, there was no reason to continue with therapy. Ben's psychiatrist concurred with this decision.

In early February, Ben got his report card. He received an incomplete in math, indicating he was continuing to have difficulty completing assignments. I had assumed the medications Ben was taking might help with his concentration and thus help him function more effectively in school, but this did not seem to be the case. Each night we would ask Ben if he had homework. Some nights he would tell us he did, and he would spend time in his room doing it. Other times he would tell us "No," and we believed him. This incomplete made me conclude Ben had been lying to us. I did not know how much I could trust my son or what to believe. I wondered how I could continue to help him work out his difficulties when I could not be sure he was being honest with me. How could I help him stay on track when I did not have the slightest way of knowing where he was with his assignments? How much of this was ADHD, how much of this was depression, and how much of this was just manipulative behavior?

I felt Ben needed to be punished in a way that would motivate him to assume responsibility. I decided to put the new ham radio he received for Christmas into our closet. He would get it back in six weeks, the end of the next grading period, if he had no incompletes. I also told him he needed to be careful not to alienate us. We were his parents who loved him; we were more committed to him than anyone else was likely to be. We needed to be able to trust him so we could help him when he got into trouble. Ben was more careful about getting his assignments done, and his ham radio was returned.

I can not remember exactly when Ben's nosebleeds began, but it was sometime that winter. In an article in the June, 1991 issue of Atlantic Monthly, Dr. Philip C. Kendall was interviewed about his work with children with depression and anxiety. A client was mentioned who had frequent headaches and nosebleeds. I found the article interesting. Did Ben's depression and anxiety have something to do with those twice a day nosebleeds?

When they began, I thought it might have something to do with wintertime dryness. Although the humidity in our house is adequate, I put a vaporizer in Ben's bedroom. When this did not help to reduce the frequency of the nosebleeds, I called our family doctor. He recommended coating the inside of Ben's nose with Vaseline, and to continue with the vaporizer. One day Ben had a particularly bad nosebleed and we made an appointment with an ear-nose-and-throat specialist. The doctor cauterized the nose, but Ben still had a nosebleed later that very night. A few weeks later, we went for a second visit to the ENT specialist, but it still did not resolve the problem.

During the winter. Ben continued his interest in horses. He did not go out to the stable as often as he had in the fall, but he did get there most weekends. As springtime approached, Ben again told me how desperately he wanted a job at the stables so he could spend more time with the horses. I got the idea of signing him up for riding lessons. He would have lots of contact with horses as well as learn about them. I hoped he would feel less helpless about waiting to be offered a job at the stables.

I saw these riding lessons as potentially helpful to Ben in a number of ways. First, working with horses was one of Ben's talents. I wanted to encourage him in anything that he was good at. Second, since he had expressed a strong desire to do work with horses, I wanted him to see that there is not just one way to get what you want in life. If one thing does not work out exactly as you planned, there are other possibilities that may turn out even better in the long run. Although a job at the stable might be good, would not riding lessons and having his own horse actually be better? Finally, since he only saw his therapist once every three weeks, would not riding every day be in it's own way therapeutic? Not only would it do him some good emotionally, but the added exercise would be helpful in lifting his mood.

The lessons were being offered through the same community schools programs as the gun safety class he had taken in fall. The more Ben thought about the lessons the more excited he became. One day he asked to see my copy of the enrollment slip so he could check the exact time and location of the first class. I took it from my purse. When he looked at the piece of paper, he saw that I had signed up for a one night class on adolescent suicide. Ben asked, "What's that for?" I explained to him how a friend of mine had called me about it. She was planning to go, and she wondered if I would be interested in it as well. My friend knew I was concerned about Ben's depression. His response to me was a very patronizing, "Really mother, I'm beyond that."

When Ben started therapy, he had mentioned how he had once held a gun to his head. At that time, his therapist had cautioned us to make sure Ben did not have hunting equipment in his room. We took this seriously and locked up the guns. She also did not want us to completely prohibit Ben's enjoyment of shooting since it seemed like such a positive way for him to spend time with his dad and his friend. Shooting was something he was good at and loved to do. Ben needed more enjoyable activities in his life, not less. We tried to make sure Ben's handling of a gun was supervised.

Our concerns in fall and winter about safety were prudent, but what Ben seemed to be saying now was that the danger had passed. With someone like Ben, however, one could not be sure. Ben felt he was emotionally better and beyond any danger of seriously hurting himself. As the spring approached, Ben did seem to be getting along better with other people. He was taking lithium and the anti-depressant (Prozac) and seeing his therapist. Sometimes when his dad would pick him up after school Ben would be in a good mood, saying he had had a great day. We were becoming closer as a family now that we could enjoy Ben's company. The four of us would have pleasant talks in the evening or have fun playing a game. Doing things like this had never been possible when Ben was overly sensitive and easily frustrated. As the highs and lows of his mood swings leveled off, he seemed to be operating in the middle range, which allowed all of us to relax and enjoy having him around.

In April, Ben started his riding lessons. He got along famously with the instructor. Ben liked adults, and the teacher was quite taken by this fourteen year old who seemed mature for his age. By his second lesson, I was already inquiring into the possibility of leasing a horse for the summer.

Everything seemed to be going well for Ben. He was settling down emotionally, he had hobbies, and he was enjoying himself. I wondered how much longer Ben would need to continue to see his psychiatrist. I hoped he could finish out the calendar year with her and then try decreasing the visits, especially during the snow-filled winter months. My perceptions of Ben as more stable may have been shared by his therapist, for in early May, she decided to discontinue the lithium on a trial basis. This is often done to discover if a medication is necessary and effective in treatment. She did not want to continue to give a medication for a long period of time without knowing for sure that Ben really needed it. Remember, from October to December of 1988 he had only been on the lithium. From December to May of 1989 he had both the antidepressant, Prozac, and the lithium. Ben was looking forward to the summer and his horse. The summer seemed like a safe time to try a reduction in medications. We would be able to see how Ben would be on the anti-depressant alone.

But several months earlier, Ben had expressed to me his fears about being taken off lithium. He felt it stabilized him and he did not want to stop taking it. When this reduction was presented, Ben said he would go along with it because it was a trial and he could go back on it. I did not have any objections to the reduction. If Ben could be helped by taking only the anti-depressant alone, I would be thrilled. After all, the lithium may have been a factor in his latest weight gain. I knew how much this boy had constantly fought the battle with the bathroom scale.

The first week of the medication reduction, Ben was to go from the three tablets of lithium per day down to two. That first week everything seemed to be going along fine. I began to think maybe we were wrong about Ben's need for lithium. It was also during that week I bought Ben a saddle for the horse we were leasing for the summer. It was one of the nicest experiences I can remember. His riding teacher had come across the saddle at a garage sale. She told us about it and said if we were interested in buying it, we could bring it out to her house and give it a test ride to see if it fit the horse and was comfortable for Ben. We followed her suggestion. The saddle was fine and we were thrilled with the purchase. In the car coming back home with it, Ben saw some young people his age and commented, "Very few kids are as lucky as I am."

Being in a playful mood, we plotted to play a trick on Garry. We would tell my husband the used saddle did not work out but we had bought a new, expensive one at the saddle shop instead. Ben played his part of the joke perfectly, and it went without a hitch. We brought in the saddle, and then laughed as we explained how we were only kidding and got this saddle at a lower price. We all had a great time. In fact, everything that first week seemed to be going smoothly.

The second week Ben was to go from two lithium tablets down to just one. Somewhere during this week we began to see some of his old problems returning, especially his difficulty settling down at night and getting to sleep. During the end of the second week Garry was going to be out of town for a conference. While he was gone we were to have house guests. I wanted one of our guests to use Ben's bedroom, which meant he would have to make it presentable. Although he made some good-natured protests, he was in a cooperative mood and he said, "Oh well, I'll just whistle while I work." He went about doing a major overhaul to his room.

When I took in the mail, I received a notice from one of his teachers. There was a possibility Ben would fail one of his classes. As long as we were overhauling his room, I had him take out his ham radio and package it up until his class work improved again. It did not seem as if he was getting his act together regarding completing assignments after all. When Ben went to school on Monday, he talked with his teacher, who was willing to work out a deal with him on how he could complete some work and pass the class.

On Wednesday night we talked, and Ben expressed unhappiness about school and his medication reduction. I encouraged him to tell his therapist exactly what was happening.

The following day Ben was supposed to start the third week of his lithium reductions, which meant he would completely stop taking it. Things were not going well, so I decided to put aside any further reduction and just have Ben stay at one tablet a day.

I thought about calling his therapist, but I felt I did not have anything concrete to say. Although we had noticed some difficulty with sleep, there had only been one night of total sleeplessness. Ben told me he could not stand being in school, but I was not sure what he meant. With no more than a general impression of his instability, I could not articulate anything objective. It made more sense to hold the lithium to one pill than to call the therapist with vague impressions. Although one tablet a day is not a therapeutic dose of lithium, giving the one daily pill might facilitate a quicker re-establishment of the medication at the full dosage. We would just wait until his regularly scheduled appointment the following week. Then the therapist could see Ben for herself and render a more objective opinion about recurring symptoms and his need for the lithium.

My weekend house guests came, and Ben seemed a little impulsive and hyperactive. While the rest of us went to my niece's graduation, Ben went with a friend to the horse stables. Having Ben on his own like that made me uneasy, and when I got back home I was relieved but also surprised to see him asleep in his bed.

The following Monday, Garry was home from his conference. I told him about the letter from his teacher, but by then we also knew there was a way to work out the failing grade. Ben's therapist had encouraged us to continue to expect Ben to do his work and to make some of the things he enjoyed contingent upon completion of his school work. Garry was trying to enforce the rule that Ben was not to go to the stables until, and unless, his school work was done. But it was hard to always get a reliable answer to the question: "Is your school work done?"

A limited amount of time remained in the school year for Ben to complete his assignments. He probably had not been doing all of his work for the last several months, even though many nights he would tell us his school work was complete. The end of the school year, the time for all assignments to be handed in, coincided with his lower dosages of lithium. At Ben's next appointment with his therapist, May 25, she could see Ben was not in as good a shape as he had been three weeks earlier. She told us to go ahead with the full therapeutic dosage of lithium immediately. The nervousness I experienced the previous two weeks was replaced with relief. Now that it was clear that Ben benefited from the medication, he would probably stay on three tablets for the rest of his life. I began to relax and to stop worrying about him.

Ben had been invited to a friend's home for Memorial Day weekend, so my husband and I had planned our own vacation. We could enjoy pursuing some of our own personal creative activities. We remarked to each other how this was the first time we could enjoy a whole weekend at our own house, on our own, since the children were born. Our daughter had left for a three week trip to Germany, and Ben was away with a friend for the weekend. We were childless and felt like newlyweds. Stopping by at Garry's sister's house while out for a walk, we reflected that we might not mind an empty nest when it came in four or five years.

On Sunday night we picked up Ben, who had a great time with his friend. He had helped their family with a building project at their home on a lake. The next morning, May 29, Ben slept late, and had his riding lesson in the afternoon. When we got there, I reminded his instructor that Thursday was June 1. We planned to be at her house after school on Thursday to ride, since it was the first official day of the lease of her horse. Ben grabbed his new saddle from the back of our car and went off to his lesson.

When he came back one hour later, his teacher expressed concern over an injury to Ben's leg. The other rider's horse had bolted and rammed up against Ben's horse. Ben came close to being pinned under the weight of both horses which would have fallen on top of him. Luckily, both riders had handled the horses fairly well and Ben's leg had only been squeezed between the horse and the wall. Everyone had been a bit shaken by the accident.

Ben had another near miss a week earlier with his bike. When riding home from the stables he had nearly been hit by a car. Looking back now, these incidents seem like a premonition of things to come. Tuesday, May 30th, Ben went to school. When he got home, he wanted to go to the stables. Garry asked Ben if he had his work done, and he told us it was finished. Ben then went to the stables with a new friend who was interested in training horses. The following day he took his life.

Why did Ben die? Did the use of the antidepressant give him back enough energy to act out on what he had been thinking about doing during his darkest mood? Dr. Klerman (1984, p. 34) tells us that "the highest suicidal mortality occurs during the six-to-nine-month period after symptomatic improvement has occurred." Ben started medication and therapy in October and died in May, seven months later. Or was his depression lifted that spring because his seasonal depression was taking its normal up turn? (Suicide rates for adolescents are somewhat higher during springtime.)

Was the discontinuation of lithium a factor? Did we inadvertently remove the stability this element can provide to a person with bipolar illness? Or was it the impulsivity of this ADHD child that caused his death? Was his suicide simply the last of a series of dangerous behaviors that typify the life of a person with ADHD? Or was his death a result of his anxiety disorder? Did Ben experience a panic attack shortly before his suicide, an attack that in effect proved fatal?

Why did Ben die? The final answer to this question will always remain a mystery.

Who is to Blame for Ben's Death

Anger is an integral part of grief. When someone precious has been taken from you, it is only natural to look around for someone or something to blame. So who is to blame for the death of my son Ben?

Was the school system at fault? I have painful memories of not being taken seriously as I voiced my opinion that Ben's inability to concentrate was a legitimate form of learning disability. I was saying these things in the early and middle 1980's, before ADD was recognized as it is today. However, I can not honestly blame any individual teacher for Ben's death. On the whole, they were simply doing a good job of what teachers were supposed to do: namely, expecting students to complete assignments. Some were truly outstanding educators.

Were Ben's medications at fault? Eight months after his death, the news media carried a report from Dr. Martin Teicher at Harvard regarding six suicides among patients taking Prozac. Was this drug a factor in Ben's death? If Prozac truly did stimulate suicide, I felt an obligation to warn others. I consulted an attorney and then a malpractice specialist. That attorney referred me to the only law office in our state that dealt with product safety cases.

Later I spent an hour on the phone with a staff member from that office, discussing the case at length. It was one of the most therapeutic conversations I'd ever had!

Surprisingly, I was able to discuss the case objectively. I was grateful to the attorney for telling me exactly what I could expect if I chose to pursue this matter. My husband had taken Ben to his last appointments with the psychiatrist, and would therefore need to testify, something that would be extremely difficult for him. Ben's psychiatrist would likely be counter-sued for malpractice, because in the fall of 1988 the new drug Prozac may not have yet carried FDA indication for use with children or adolescents. Although Prozac is safe to use with that age group, the technicalities of the FDA requirements could have been used against her. Since the use of Prozac was a result of a collaborative decision between us and the psychiatrist, the idea of a potential law suit against her was abhorrent.

My potential suit grew from a concern for the safety of the product and a sense of obligation to others. The lawyer assured me that if Prozac did in fact stimulate suicide, the scientific community will determine this; I need not feel personally responsible. Research has now clearly demonstrated that Prozac and the other SSRI's (Selective Serotonine Re-uptake Inhibitors) do not stimulate suicide. The only drug that appears to stimulate suicide is alcohol.

What is the role of any anti-depressant in suicide? The recovery from depression is not like the recovery from a broken bone or an infection. Instead of a gradual but straightforward improvement, recovery from depression has a saw-tooth pattern. After starting medication, the patient will often feel better within several weeks. This initial reduction of symptoms is usually followed by a temporary dip once again into depression, as the brain fights back from the medications' attempt to bring the person back to normal mood. This descent back into depression can be a particularly dangerous time. To feel bad again after feeling better is disappointing and reinforces the feelings of hopelessness.

Close friends, family members, and the patients themselves need to know about the saw-tooth pattern of recovery. They will then know that temporary dips into depression do not necessarily mean the medication isn't working, but recovery from depression takes this jagged course. Unfortunately, family and friends are often so worn out from trying to cope with the condition prior to receiving medication that they may become overly relieved once treatment begins. They make the assumption that now that the case is in the hands of a professional, the danger is past. We usually do not make that kind of assumption about a patient with a cancer or heart condition, and. it is an error to make that kind of assumption for a person with serious depression.

Dr. Fredrick Goodwin made a simple mathematical calculation. He took the number of persons who were taking Prozac for depression during a particular year and multiplied it by the number of people with severe depression who make a serious attempt to complete suicide in any given year - (3.5%). Seventy-five thousand attempts is what one could expect if Prozac did not have any effect in decreasing suicide. The number of reported attempts by Prozac users that year was only five hundred; the FDA believes they may only actually receive reports of 1/10 of actual attempts. So the real number of attempts may be as high as five thousand. However, 5,000 is significantly fewer than the 75,000 that would be expected if Prozac had no effect in deterring suicide attempts.

In objective terms Prozac can not be targeted for blame in my son's death. I especially do not doubt the wisdom of Ben's psychiatrist for trying this medication with him. In 1988, Prozac may not have yet received FDA approval for use by children, but experienced psychiatrists know that the challenges facing them can not always wait for the time-consuming and often financially prohibitive process of getting a medicine approved through the FDA for every possible use. Dr. Fredrick Goodwin, past-president of the National Institute of Mental Health, has said that psychiatrists who exclusively adhere only to universal conventions are, by definition, practicing yesterday's medicine.

Was Ben's therapist at fault for the trial discontinuation of the lithium? We took Ben to a specialist in child and adolescent psychiatry for what we believed to be bipolar illness. Lithium is one of the standard treatments for manic depressive illness. It has an excellent track record of decreasing suicide, and Ben died during a physician ordered trial reduction/elimination of the lithium. Was her decision to take Ben off that medicine unwise? Let's look at the case from the scientific perspective of the 1990's.

Bipolar illness manifests several different patterns. One is the MDI (mania, depression, inter-episode recovery) form, in which the patient's first experience with the illness is a manic high. Untreated, the mania can last up to four months, and often the patient descends into a depression that can last up to twelve months. The patient will then be free of symptoms for several years, until another mood swing occurs. Patients with an MDI pattern typically respond well to lithium.

Other bipolar patients have the DMI (depression, mania, inter-episode recovery) pattern. Their experience of the illness starts first with one or even several episodes of depression. Because depression is their only symptom, it may be assumed that they have unipolar depression. The manic high comes later. They too will have periods of time when they are totally free of their symptoms. Patients with the DMI pattern often do not respond as well to lithium. Evidence is beginning to show that DMI patients may respond better to seizure medications such as Depakote (valproic acid) or Tegretol (carbamazapine), or a combination of the two.

Ben was not responding well to lithium. In my opinion, he had the DMI pattern. Seizure medications may have stabilized his mood better than lithium. However, Ben was treated in late 1988 and early 1989, before the use of seizure medication for persons with bipolar illness was well known.

Not only was Ben not responding very well to lithium; he was also experiencing significant weight gain. His visits to the pediatric cardiologist showed our concern for this child with a family history of heart disease. Ben also had tremors from the lithium. Presently it is common medical knowledge that tremors can be easily treated with a beta blocker, but it is unfair to judge 1988 care by current standards. Lithium also can cause some decreased ability to concentrate. Ben's ADD is characterized by problems with concentration -- another reason that psychiatrists now would rather use a seizure medication like Depakote for children and adolescents. If a young person suffers with the MDI pattern and does respond to lithium, some psychiatrists may recommend lower dosages of lithium in combination with Depakote.

In my opinion, Ben's psychiatrist did the best she could with the information she had available to her at that time. She was dealing with a complex case. Physicians who work with difficult problems should not be persecuted when things do not turn out as well as they would have expected.

I believe Ben's first episode happened during the first week in June, 1980, when he wet the bed three nights in a row. He killed himself on May 31, 1989. There is a seasonal factor in depressive illness. For bipolar patients, the switch period from winter depression into summer mania is a particularly dangerous time. The patient's energy level increases without a complete elimination of the depressive mood. This produces enough energy to do what they have been thinking about -- killing themselves! This switch period is especially dangerous for patients who suffer from mixed states.

Psychologist Dr. Kay Jamison writes, "Mixed states represent a critical combination of dysphoric mood (anxiety plus depression), depressed thought combined with an exceptionally perturbed, agitated and unpleasant physical state that is usually accompanied by a heightened energy level and increased impulsivity." (Lifesaver, Summer, 1994) Data indicates that 40% of people with bipolar illness experience mixed states. The percentage is even higher (approaching 65%) for persons with an early-onset of the illness. There is a high rate of attempted suicide during mixed states. I believe Ben suffered from mixed states and because he had early onset illness, the odds are that I am right.

Am I to blame for my son's death? That is the question most parents of suicide victims ask themselves. I personally do not feel guilt about Ben's death. If I had not received the powerful message   "This was supposed to happen this day," I might have been tempted to blame myself. But I did have that experience and I am grateful for it.

If there is a guilty parent, she is Mother Nature. Depression is a biological illness. Manic depressive illness is particularly identified as a genetic illness.   It has an especially high suicide risk factor. Twenty-five percent of persons not treated with stabilizing medications (lithium or the seizure medications) or those few unfortunate people who have a treatment-resistant case (who do not respond to any medication) die by suicide. I was surprised to learn that manic depressive illness is now considered to be more lethal than childhood leukemia. This is especially meaningful to me.   I have a dear friend whose daughter had childhood leukemia when she was five years old. The daughter is thankfully alive. Our son's first episode with manic depressive illness dates from his wetting incidents at age five.   Our son is not alive. Psychiatrists may recognize the high risk of   serious depression illness, but others often do not.   Cancer patients are so obviously sick; bipolar children and adolescents have a biological illness that is not so obvious.

Mother Nature perhaps is to blame, but I am not personally angry with her either. She is the source of my son's illness, but she is also the creator of everything of beauty in our world. She may have caused his death, but she also gave him life.

In the final analysis, I do not blame anyone for Ben's death. I certainly do not blame him.

Contents - Appendix 1

I. Screening instrument for Fourth - Sixth Grade.

II Recommended curriculum for 7th - 12th Grade

A. For Parents, Teachers, and Health Professionals

1. Psychiatric disorders of almost all suicide completers
2. Differences between suicide attempters and completers
3. Stressors proceeding most adolescent suicide attempts
4. Symptom changes
5. Conditions commonly accompanying depression
6. How adolescents can help one another
7. Self-help for depressed youth

B. Especially for Health Professionals

1. Recommendations to the media - Things to Avoid
2. Seasonal variations on suicide rates
3. General treatment goals for depressed youth
4. Crisis intervention for depressed persons
5. Modified hypoglycemic diet for persons on lithium

Note: Some of this material was obtained from a workshop presented by Dr. H. Hoberman on adolescent suicide.

I Instrument for Fourth - Sixth Grade

	Most of the time	Sometimes	Never
I look forward to things as much as I used to			
I sleep very well			
I feel like crying			
I like to go out to play			
I feel like running away			
I get stomach aches			
I have lots of energy			
I enjoy my food			
I can stick up for myself			
I think life isn't worth living			
I am good at things I do			
I enjoy the things I do as much as I used to			
I like talking with my family			
I have horrible dreams			
I feel very lonely			
I am easily cheered up			
I feel so sad I can hardly stand it			
I feel very bored			

Request for reprints to Dr. P. Birleson, The Young People's Unit, Tiperline House, Tipperline Road, Edinburgh EH105HF, U.K.

The term "depressive disorder" refers to depression that is serious enough to impairs a person's ability to function for a period of time, usually at least a number of weeks. This would exclude temporary grief reactions, normal moods shifts, demoralization, and the presence of ongoing personality traits.

Demoralization is different from pure depression disorder in that it is not as pervasive. Children who are demoralized can still enjoy themselves some of the time, sleep normally, and do not experience unusual appetite. Although they too may develop a sense of hopelessness and show signs of sadness, demoralization is often seen as either secondary to other psychiatric conditions or as a normal reaction to failure.

One can easily imagine a continuum from normal mood through demoralization to severe clinical depression. Think of another continuum with normal mood, proceeding to the common mild state of depressive that does not significantly impair functioning in one's environment, toward moderate depression which does reduce efficient functioning, ending with severe depression in which impairment is serious.

The depression scale for children was tested by comparing data from various groups of children.

1. Youngsters who were referred to the department of child psychiatry in a hospital because of clinical depression

2. Two sets of youngsters who had psychological/behavioral problems but were not diagnosed as suffering primarily from depression

3. Youngsters from a local elementary school

This self-rating instrument, by definition, does not need to be given by a psychiatrist. Because it is in the public domain, its use if not restricted. It can easily be given to any child or group of children. Because many youngsters experience depression starting as young as 4th grade, the best strategy would be to start screening then, do it several times each year, and keep a simple record of the results for future comparisons. Responses were numericalized by scoring Most of the time - 0, Sometimes - 1, Never - 2

To my knowledge there are no guidelines that differentiate the various levels of depression by specific ranges in the scores. What is known is that none of the youngsters from the local elementary school scored over 11. An examination of the data from the groups indicate that a score of 13 or above is likely to be reasonably indicative of "depressive disorder," although there may be an acceptable false positive or false negative of less than 20%.

It may be prudent to suggest that youngsters with very low scores do not experience any level of depression, and children whose scores approach 10 may suffer from mild or moderate depression. Since the ability to concentrate and remember is affected by depression, these milder forms of depression interfere with their ability to perform in school as well as their teachers, their parents, and they themselves would like. Even milder forms of depression deserve attention. Any child whose score is 11 or above should be refered to mental health professionals for further assessment.

II. Recommended Curriculum for 7th - 12th Grade

Dr. David Burns' *Ten Days To Self-Esteem* contains an easy to use depression checklist and an anxiety inventory. The scoring is easily accomplished, enabling students to see for themselves how they are doing. Burns provides a scoring key for the various levels of depression and anxiety. In the 1993 edition, a score of 0 - 4 = no depression, 5 - 10 = normal but unhappy, 11 - 20 = mild depression, 21 - 30 = moderate, 31 - 45 = severe.

Burns' text was designed as a workbook to help people who suffer from depression and anxiety. Pioneered and tested at the Presbyterian Medical Center at Philadelphia, careful research establishes its effectiveness. A leaders manual is also available, enabling classroom teachers who are willing to master this curriculum to use cognitive techniques efficiently with groups.

In the next few years I intend to publish a book entitled *Suicide Prevention: Can It Be Done?*-- a natural extension of the workshop I now present using the same title. It examines all of the factors top researchers in the field have identified as putting someone at high risk for suicide.

The content of that unpublished work is more inclusive than the chapters here that focus primarily on depression and anxiety. The new book has specific chapters on learning disabilities (especially ADHD), alcohol and drug abuse, and personality disorders (especially borderline personality and antisocial personality). It is my belief that ultimately these factors need to included in an elective class for grade 7 - 12. However, since depression and anxiety remain the single most important risk factors, the workbook *Ten Days To Self-Esteem* and the material covered here in *Depression in the Young* give a genuinely useful working foundation that will help the majority of youngsters.

A.1 PSYCHIATRIC DISORDER

Almost all suicide completers have a psychiatric disorder.

1. Depressive disorder

2. Bipolar disorder

3. Alcohol or drug abuse

4. Antisocial behavior

5. Attention Deficit-Hyperactivity Disorder

A.2 DIFFERENCES BETWEEN ADOLESCENT SUICIDE ATTEMPTERS AND COMPLETERS

1. Gender

> More females attempt than do males
> (ratio of at least 10 to 1)

> More males complete than do females
> (ratio of approximately 5 to 1)

2. Availability of firearms

Suicide completion is at least four times more likely in a home in which firearms are accessible.

A.3 STRESSORS

Attempters have two times as many negative life events in the last six months: a greater number of negative life events in their lifetime.

1. Breakup with boy/girlfriend

2. Trouble with sibling

3. Change in family financial status

4. Parents' divorce

5. Losing close friend

6. Trouble with teacher

7. Change to a new school

8. Personal illness or injury

9. Failing grades

10. Increased arguments with parents

Stressors: Loss and conflict

A.4 SYMPTOMS CHANGE AS DEPRESSED CHILDREN REACH ADOLESCENCE AND YOUNG ADULTHOOD

A. Symptoms that decrease with age

1. Depressed appearance

2. Self-esteem problems

3. Somatic complaints

4. Hallucinations

B. Symptoms that remain stable with age

1. Depressed mood

2. Poor concentration

3. Insomnia

4. Suicidal thoughts and attempts

C. Symptoms that increase with age

1. Anhedonia - (inability to experience pleasure)

2. Diurnal mood - (feeling worse in morning than later in the day)

3. Hopelessness

4. Psychomotor retardation - slowed speech

5. Definitive delusions - illogical assumptions about oneself or others

A.5   LIST OF CONDITIONS COMMONLY ACCOMPANYING DEPRESSION

Only 25% of children and adolescents have depression alone. 75% have at least one other (co-morbid) condition

A. External Disorder - problems easily seen by and bothersome to other people.

   1.   ADHD (inattention, impulsive, overactive)

   2.   Conduct Disorder (cannot follow rules at home and at school)

   3.   Learning Disabilities (Dyslexia - can not read, spell or learn a foreign language; dyscalcula - cannot do math)

   4.   Delinquency - involvement with law enforcement

B. Internal Disorders - Problems that are internally painful to the person, but not necessarily troublesome to others

   1.   Anxiety Disorder - shortness of breath, dizziness, a sinking feeling in the stomach, and rapid heartbeat

   2.   Eating Disorder - anorexia, bulimia, obesity

   3.   Substance Abuse - the beginnings of alcoholism and/or drug addiction

A.6   HOW ADOLESCENTS CAN HELP ONE ANOTHER

1. Care about your friends; be available and listen

2. Explore possible solutions to problems, but don't tell friends what to do.

3. Try to understand without judging, arguing, denying, or minimizing feelings.

4. Tolerate depressed, irritable moods

5. Help to remember good things about them and their life.

6. Emphasize that they can live through deep hurt and that there are people who care.

7. Explore what things they can look forward to.

8. Reach out to fringe kids.

9. Maintain confidence, but if really worried about suicide, don't take chance - alert responsible adult.

A.7   SELF-HELP FOR DEPRESSED YOUTH

1. Try to understand if particular things are making you depressed.

2. Tell someone you trust how you feel - express yourself and get feelings out.

3. If necessary, write out feelings.

4. Be with other people, even if hard; avoid being alone.

5. Exercise - be physically active.

6. Do at least one thing you really enjoy, even if you don't want to do it.

7. Find something you did well or were satisfied with and praise yourself

8. Look your best.

9. Get out of the house and do something.

A.9 POSSIBLE SIGNS OF DISTRESSED YOUTH OUT OF CLASSROOM

1. Overhearing remarks indicative of significant unhappiness or despair.

2. Knowledge that prized possessions are being given away.

3. Loss of interest in extracurricular activities.

4. Direct suicide threats or attempts.

5. Marked emotionality.

6. Recent depression to suicidal behavior in family.

7. Recent conflict or losses in close relationships.

8. Increased and heavy use of alcohol or drugs

B. 1 RECOMMENDATIONS TO THE MEDIA

1. *Avoid* oversimplifying the many factors that cause the suicide

2. *Avoid* sensationalizing the suicide

3. *Avoid* glorifying the victim

4. *Avoid* making the suicide appear to be a rewarding experience or an appropriate or effective tool to achieve a personal gain

5. *Avoid* depicting the method of the suicide

6. *Avoid* emphasis to stressor or simplistic psychological presses as much as pressures

7 *Avoid* massive or repeated doses of press coverage

B 2 SEASONAL VARIATIONS ON SUICIDE RATES
Effect of light on persons with depressive illness

People who have bipolar I or major depression (typical pattern) along with impulsive/aggressive behavior are affected by rate of change in the ratio of light VS darkness. The times when change is fastest is during the spring and fall.

People who have bipolar II and others with the atypical pattern are effected by the amount of light. Summer daylight is twice as long as winter daylight. Atypical clients often have winter depression and summer hypomania. They are especially at risk during switch from depression into hypomania.

Spring has higher rate of suicide. October also shows elevated risk but not as high as March - June.

Monthly Peak Occurrences of Suicide
a review based on 61 studies (Number indicate data points)

Jan 1
Feb 1
Mar 7
April 11
May 20
June 8
July 1
Aug 1
Sep   0.5
Oct 6
Nov 3
Dec 4

B.3   GENERAL TREATMENT GOALS FOR DEPRESSED YOUTH

1. Manage immediate stressors.

2. Manage depressive symptoms.

3. Manage symptoms of co-morbid disorders.

4. Reduce impairing depressive symptoms.

5. Reduce chronic stressors, including family dysfunction and disorder.

6. Teach or enhance competencies and coping skills.

7. Deepen social relationships and expand social network.

8. Explore psychological conflicts and core pathogenic beliefs.

9. Facilitate disconfirming experiences for hopelessness and core pathogenic beliefs.

10. Create mechanisms for generalization and relapse prevention

B.4 CRISIS INTERVENTION FOR DISTRESSED PERSONS

1. Make psychological contact; establish relationship

   - create opportunity to talk privately
   - encourage talking
   - listen
   - be emphatic; communicate concern
   - clarify and summarize facts and feelings

2. Explore dimensions of crisis/problem

   - deal with immediate present
   - focus on precipitating event
   - facilitate awareness of person's reactions to stressor
   - evaluate coping (e.g., lack of inappropriate coping)
   - identify immediate needs, then eventual needs
   - access suicide risk

3. Re-conceptualize meaning of crisis

   - restate/reframe situation
   - develop linkage between low self-esteem, current stressor
   - ineffective coping, and hopelessness
   - relate crisis to problem in current roles and relationships

4. Examine possible solutions

   - what solutions already attempted
   - brainstorm other alternatives to meeting needs
   - emphasize and mobilize person's strengths and
   - competencies

5. Assist in taking specific, concrete action

- problem-oriented and/or protection plan
- harness existing or previously effective coping strategies
- give advice
- involve significant others and utilize support network

6. Follow-up
- contract
- arrange procedure
- emphasize caring

B.5 MODIFIED HYPOGLYCEMIC DIET FOR PERSONS ON LITHIUM

The recommendations here are generally applicable for persons who experience weight gain on lithium. Specific recommendations for individuals should be obtained by a dietitian in cooperation with physician orders.

1. Avoid simple (refined) carbohydrates that involve high levels of sugar,

2. Increase complex carbohydrates such as breads, cereals and vegetables,

3. Increase high fiber foods such as fruits, vegetables and grains,

4. Decrease fat in your diet,

5. Eat a number of small meals and healthy snacks between meals.

NOTE:

This short list sounds like everything you have been hearing in the last years about what constitutes a healthy diet to decrease the risk of heart disease and cancer. Consequently, the person on lithium simply needs to eat a generally healthy diet.

WORKS CITED

Adolescent stress and depression. (1986). Teens in distress. University of Minnesota: Minnesota Extension Service.

Ardrey, R. (1961). African genesis: A personal investigation into the animal origins and nature of man. New York: Dell Publishing Co., Inc.

Burns, D.D., M.D. (1980). Feeling good: The new mood therapy. New York: Signet Books.

Campbell, J. (1990). Transformations of myth through time. New York: Harper & Row.

Campbell Joseph & Bill Moyer, (1988), The Power of Myth. New York: Doubleday Dell Publishing Group Inc.

Diagnostic and Statistical Manual of Mental Disorders, Fourth Edition (1994) Washington DC: American Psychiatric Association.

Fawcett, J.A., MD (1991). Understanding the new risk factors for suicide. Lifesavers: The Newsletter of the American Suicide Foundation, 3:3.

Fawcett, J.A., MD (1992). Short- and long-term predictors of suicide in depressed patients. Lifesavers: The Newsletter of the American Suicide Foundation.

Fieve, F.R., MD (1975). Moodswings. New York: Bantam Books.

Fishman, K.D. (1991, June). Therapy for children. The Atlantic Monthly, pp. 47-69.

Gawain, S. (1978). Creative Visualizations. New York: Bantam Books.

Gelman, D. (1987, May 4). Depression. Newsweek. pp. 48-57.

Gold, M.S. (1987). The good news about depression. New York: Bantam Books.

Goode, E. (1990, March 5). Beating depression. U.S. News & World Report, pp. 48-55.

Hoberman, H.M., Ph.D. (1989). Completed suicide in children and adolescents: A review. In B.D. Garfinkel (Ed.), Adolescent suicide: Recognition, treatment, and prevention. New York: Haworth.

Jamison, K. (1994) Suicide and Manic-Depressive Illness, Lifesavers: The Newsletter of the American Suicide Foundation. 6:3

Klerman, G., Weissman, M., Rounsaville, B., & Chevron, E. (1984). Interpersonal psychotherapy of depression. New York: Basic Books, Inc.

McKay, M. & Fanning, P. (1987). Self esteem. Oakland, California: New Harbinger Publications.

McKnew, D.H., Cytryn, L., & Yahraes, H. (1983). Why isn't Johnny crying? Coping with depression in children. New York: Norton & Company.

Physicians' Desk Reference (1993) Montvale, N.J.: Medical Economics Company Inc.

Popper, C., MD (1989). Diagnosing bipolar vs. ADHD, American Academy of Child and Adolescent Psychiatry News. Washington DC

Roy, A., (1992). Schizophrenia and suicide. Lifesavers: The Newsletter of the American Suicide Foundation. 4:1

Sargent, M. (1989 a). Depressive illnesses: Treatment brings new hope. U.S. Department of Health and Human Services. National Institute of Mental Health.

Sheehan, D.V. (1983). The anxiety disease. New York: Bantam Books.

Stevens, A. (1989). The roots of war: A Jungian perspective. New York: Paragon House.

Supporting young people following a suicide. (1986) Teens in distress. University of Minnesota: Minnesota Extension Service.

Understanding the new risk factors for suicide. (1991, Summer). Lifesavers: The Newsletter of the American Suicide Foundation.

Useful information on suicide. (1986). U.S. Department of Health and Human Services. National Institute of Mental Health.

Weissman, M., Ph.D. (1991). Panic and suicidal behavior. Lifesavers: The Newsletter of the American Suicide Foundation.

FURTHER REFERENCES

Beck, Rush, Shaw and Emery, Cognitive Therapy of Depression (1979) Guilford Press, New York.

Elmer-Dewitt, P. (1992, July 6). Depression: The growing role of drug therapies. Time, pp. 57-59.

Gorman, J.M., MD (1990) The Essential Guide to Psychiatric Drugs. New York: St. Martin's Press.

Hewett, J.H. (1980). After suicide. Philadelphia, Pennsylvania: The Westminster Press.

Kubler-Ross, Elisabeth. (1975). Death, the final growth stage. Prentice-Hall, Inc., Englewood Cliff, NJ

Larson, D.E., MD (Ed.). (1990). Mayo Clinic family health book. New York: William Morrow and Company, Inc.

Sargent, M. (1990). Helping the depressed person get treatment. U.S. Department of Health and Human Services. National Institute of Mental Health.

Sarnoff Schiff, H. (1977). The bereaved parent. NY: Penguin Books.

Supporting distressed young people. (1985). Teens in distress. University of Minnesota: Minnesota Extension Service.

Teen suicide. (1985). Teens in distress. University of Minnesota: Minnesota Extension Service.

Veninga, R.L. (1985). A gift of hope: How we survive our tragedies. New York: Ballantine Books.

Wrobleski, A. (1991). Suicide survivors: A guide for those left behind. Minneapolis, Minnesota: Afterwords Publishing.

Youth Suicide Prevention Programs: A Resource Guide, National Center for Injury Prevention and Control, Centers for Disease Control, Mailstop F-36, 4770 Buford Highway NE, Atlanta, GA 30341

130

INDEX

ABOUT THE AUTHOR

Trudy Carlson never intended to write this book. Ben's death made her put aside her other writing in order to tell the story of his life. She wanted to record everything about the problems she observed during the various stages of his life, all the things she did to help him and the attempt to obtain treatment for his condition.

As she worked she discovered she had four separate topics. The first became the book, The Suicide of My Son: A Story of Childhood Depression. This is now also published as two separate works: Ben's Story and Depression in the Young.

Learning Disabilities: How to Recognize & Manage Learning & Behavioral Problems in Children   contrasts Ben's ADD (Attention Deficit Disorder) with her own personal struggle with a mild case of dyslexia. She explains why she was able to manage her problem and why Ben's was overwhelming.

Tragedy, Finding a Hidden Meaning: How to Transform the Tragedies in Your Life into Personal Growth, explores the personal and spiritual growth that can emerge from loss. "Meaning makes most things endurable, perhaps everything."

Suicide Survivors Handbook: A Guide for the Bereaved and Those Who Wish to Help Them, deals with the major issues confronting the survivor. It also gives a wealth of suggestions on what is most helpful during recovery from grief.

IMPORTANT ADDRESSES

American Foundation For Suicide Prevention
120 Wall Street
22nd Floor
New York, NY   10005
(212)363-3500

The Compassionate Friends
P.O. Box 3696
Oak Brook, IL   60522-3696

American Association of Suicidology
Suite 310
4201 Connecticut Ave., NW
Washington, DC   20008

Friends For Survival Inc.
P. O. Box 214463
Sacramento CA   95821

ORDER FORM

Telephone orders: Call Toll Free: 1-800-296-7163
Please have your Visa or MasterCard number ready
Postal Orders: Benline Press, 118 N. 60th Ave E.
                Duluth, MN. 55804
Please send the following books. I understand that I may return any
books for a full refund -- for any reason, no questions asked.

Suicide Survivor's Handbook: A Guide to the Bereaved and
Those Who Wish to Help Them $14.95 _____

Depression in the Young: What We Can do
To Help Them $9.95 _____

Tragedy, Finding a Hidden Meaning: How to Transform
the Tragedies in Your Life into Personal Growth $14.95 _____

Learning Disabilities: How to Recognize and Manage,
Learning and Behavioral Problems in Children $14.95 _____

Sales Tax: Please add 6.5% for books shipped to Minnesota addresses

_____

Shipping: Book Rate: $2.00 for the first book and 75 cents for
each additional book (Surface shipping may take three
to four weeks)   Airmail: $3.50 per book

                                    Total   _____

Payment: __ check __ credit card
Card Number:_____
Name on card:_____ Exp. Date ____/_____